I08157789

Advance Praise for
Star-Spangled Blessings

"Making America great again is possible if its people return to the One who has graced our nation with abundance and blessings. If we as a people will turn our hearts to Almighty God, He will put peace in our hearts as we reach out to bless others. Todd Starnes and Michelle Cox shed a light on the pillars and legacy of the United States—God, Family, and Freedom. *Star-Spangled Blessings* is for patriot families. Gather round and learn from history and look to the future as our nation prepares to celebrate 250 years of one nation under God."

—Franklin Graham, President and CEO, Samaritan's Purse and the Billy Graham Evangelistic Association

"*Star-Spangled Blessings* is a wonderful primer for patriots who want to embrace the faith of our Founding Fathers."

—Dr. Robert Jeffress, pastor of
First Baptist Church Dallas

"This little book is packed with big stories about how God has blessed our nation. Todd and Michelle's daily devotions are celebrations and testimonies of how prayerful patriots embraced faith and freedom to make America great!"

—Gov. Mike Huckabee

"Through time, God and country have always been linked. The founding fathers called on the Lord. They were passionate about building this country because of their faith and they accomplished miraculous things through Him. In this heartfelt devotional, you, too, will draw closer to our Savior and find new ways to imagine how He might use you."

—*New York Times* Bestselling author Karen Kingsbury

"Todd and Michelle bring rich examples of faith in God and country to life through the ancient and modern. It will give you chills and leave you inspired and encouraged to make yourself, your family, and your country better in Christ. Your heart and soul will overflow!"

—Caleb Parke, Newsmax correspondent

"Todd Starnes and Michelle Cox bring their signature blend of artful storytelling, keen insight, and patriotic conviction to *Star-Spangled Blessings*. This stirring devotional weaves history, faith, and personal anecdotes into a call to cherish our freedoms and stand boldly for biblical truth in this land. If you're looking for a blend of encouragement, inspiration, and a renewed love for God and country, this is the book for you."

—Dr. Paul Chappell, Pastor of Lancaster Baptist Church and President of West Coast Baptist College, Lancaster, CA

STAR ★ SPANGLED BLESSINGS

DEVOTIONS FOR PATRIOTS

Also by Todd Starnes

Twilight's Last Gleaming: Can America Be Saved?
Culture Jihad: How to Stop the Left from Killing a Nation

Also by Todd Starnes and Michelle Cox

Our Daily Biscuit: Devotions with a Drawl

Star ★ Spangled Blessings

Devotions for Patriots

TODD STARNES & MICHELLE COX

A POST HILL PRESS BOOK
ISBN: 979-8-89565-174-2
ISBN (eBook): 979-8-89565-175-9

Star-Spangled Blessings:
Devotions for Patriots

Cover Design by Joseph Huntley

Post Hill Press
New York • Nashville
posthillpress.com

Published in the United States of America

3 4 5 6 7 8 9 10

Dedicated to the great patriots who work hard every day to make America great.
—Todd Starnes

Dedicated to our beloved United States of America. To those who came before us and left us a legacy of faith and an amazing country. And to my precious grandchildren: Anna, Jack, Ava, Eden, Ethan, Nolan, Hank, Reese, Duke, Mason, and Oakley. Carry that legacy of faith and freedom to another generation.
—Michelle Cox

"Blessed is the nation whose God is the Lord."
—Psalm 33:12a (KJV)

Contents

Introduction: Our Star-Spangled Blessings

I've often wondered what our Founding Fathers would think of their great American experiment. Imagine George Washington strolling down the Las Vegas Strip or Thomas Jefferson riding the "Tennessee Tornado" at Dollywood. Think of John Adams catching a "throwed roll" at Lambert's Café in Missouri.

I wonder if they would be awestruck by the fireworks in New York City on the Fourth of July or if they would cheer at the Super Bowl. Would they marvel at the soaring Gateway Arch in St. Louis and the majesty of the Rocky Mountains? Would Betsy Ross wash down a MoonPie with an RC Cola?

On the last day of the Constitutional Convention of 1787, Benjamin Franklin was asked if we had a republic or a monarchy?

"A republic, if you can keep it," he replied.

There is no doubt that America is the most exceptional nation in the world. In the face of great adversity and insurmountable odds, we have overcome. And we have been blessed.

That's really the theme of this patriotic devotional: to reflect on those star-spangled blessings.

That's not to say that our great nation has not been through some squabbles. There have been more than a few—and some were doozies. We've made lots of mistakes, but we've also righted many wrongs.

Perseverance. This is a word that has defined us over the years. Franklin Delano Roosevelt announcing to the nation about "a date which will live in infamy." Walter Cronkite delivering a news bulletin from Dallas, Texas. President George W. Bush standing on the pile of rubble at Ground Zero with a bullhorn.

Yet, in the midst of great tragedy, our nation has always found strength in Almighty God—our defender and our protector.

President Trump knows of that strength, that divine intervention. He survived not one, but two assassination attempts.

During a speech in 2024, Trump said, "Many people have told me that God spared my life for a reason, and that reason was to save our country and to restore

America to greatness. And now we are going to fulfill that mission together."

I vividly recall watching as the shots rang out in Butler County, Pennsylvania. My heart stopped as Trump dropped to the stage. But then, he rose up and—with blood streaming down his face—he thrust his fist into the air, shouting, "Fight, fight, fight!"

President Trump would then urge Americans to read their Bibles, get back to church, and pray.

"Let's make America pray again," he voiced.

It's that sort of American spirit that has resonated with people across the fruited plain. These are moments that define us as a nation.

Our little book is packed with big stories about why this nation is the most exceptional country in the world.

Each chapter includes a prayer for patriots, a liberty lesson to inspire you to take action, and what we like to call a "Yankee Doodle"—some practical questions to help you apply our devotions to your daily life. I suspect you will discover that our Yankee Doodles are indeed dandy!

We've also added a few recipes for your next Fourth of July gathering, church "dinner on the grounds," or neighborhood potluck. Take time to gather with your fellow Americans and celebrate our great country and our faith.

Lee Greenwood is a dear friend of mine and his anthem to the land of the free and the home of the brave still brings a tear to my eye as I write these words from the hills of Tennessee.

I suspect that if our Founding Fathers were here today, they would love this land from sea to shining sea. And they would join their fellow countrymen in asking God to bless the USA.

So, pour yourself a glass of lemonade, settle into your front porch swing, and discover our nation's star-spangled blessings.

CHAPTER ONE

A Flickering Flame

"Return to me, says the Lord of hosts,
and I will return to you..."
—Zechariah 1:3b (ESV)

A few years back, I spent many months researching our family heritage. The process was like putting a giant jigsaw puzzle together. I found fascinating details, photos of our ancestors, old letters and stories that brought tears to my eyes, and discovered family members who'd come from Ireland, Holland, Wales, and many other places.

But the one thing that stood out more than anything else was the legacy of faith that had been handed down from one set of ancestors to the next. There were precious stories of great-great-grandparents who—with their final breaths—prayed for their children, grandchildren, and future generations.

There were reports of family members who fought bravely for our country, protecting our freedoms and their loved ones, and records of numerous men and women who'd helped start and build churches that impacted their communities for generations.

They were faithful—to God and to country—and because of their steadfast faithfulness, I had the privilege of growing up in a country where we would pledge allegiance to the flag at school each morning and where (yes, even in public schools) our teachers taught us Bible verses and stories that built character in us.

Over the past few years, I've grieved as our freedoms have started slipping away from us. I've seen attacks and derision against God and faith. I've watched as chaos and hatred have filled our beloved country.

And you know what absolutely broke my heart? My generation—*our* generation—is the one that allowed the flame of faith to flicker across our great land. Fellow patriot, we can't let that flame go out. It's not too late to make it shine brightly again, to return to the God who made our country great. The future of our nation, our children, and our grandchildren depends on it.

We find the answer in 2 Chronicles 15:4 (NIV), "But in their distress they turned to the Lord, the God of Israel, and sought him, and he was found by them."

God tells us in Deuteronomy 28:8 (ESV), "The Lord will command the blessing on you in your barns and in all that you undertake. And he will bless you in the land that the Lord your God is giving you."

Dear friend, I don't want to be the generation where the flame of faith burns out. It's time for us to come together and take a stand for God, our country, and our families. Let's make that flame burn brightly again. We must.

Yankee Doodle

1. What are some of the ways in which my generation has failed to hand down our faith to this latest generation?
2. What do I personally need to do to help bring our country back to God? To protect our freedoms? To protect our heritage of faith?
3. How can I help fan the flame of faith so it will shine brightly across the fruited plain?
4. How can I inspire others to join me in this important task?

Patriot Prayer

Dear Father,

Thank You for those who came before us who were faithful to leave us a heritage of a country where we could worship You freely. Thank You for those who have fought for our country—and have even given their lives—so that we could enjoy those freedoms. We don't deserve Your mercy, but we sure do need it. We ask Your forgiveness for how we haven't let our lights shine brightly for You. This land we love has become a dark place because of it. We ask You to restore our country and to bring us back to You. Give us courage and strength, because if we don't take a stand for You and for our country, who will?

Amen.

Friends, we no longer have the option of just standing back and watching as our country implodes from within. We can't be bystanders as more vocal groups work to take away the things that are precious to us and to America. We are in a battle for the soul of our country. Fellow warriors, today is the time for us to take a good look at our souls. To ask God to shine a light on things we need to fix—because we can't work on anything else until we fix us first. To repent where there's a need. To turn back to God with focus and a commitment to be as faithful as those who came before us. Our country, our children and grandchildren, and future generations are depending on us.

CHAPTER TWO

God Bless America

"I will make you a great nation;
I will bless you and make your name great;
and you shall be a blessing."
—Genesis 12:2 (NKJV)

God has blessed America. Immensely. With all our faults and failures, we've been the greatest country on the planet. We've been the beacon on the hill. The example to the world. The friend to many nations. The helping hand to those who've needed it.

America has been the dream for people around the world. They've worked. Scrimped. Saved. Jumped through the hoops of immigration. And imagined the day when they, too, could become an American citizen and enjoy the blessings that we so often take for granted.

God has given us a land that is stunning in its diverse beauty. Where our fertile soil has yielded a bounty of food for our tables—and more to share.

God has blessed us with opportunities. America has been the place where someone could start with nothing in their pockets or bank accounts, but with sacrifice, ingenuity, and hard work, they could provide a great life for their families—and even become millionaires.

Where others around the world have lived with oppression, we've lived safely and free. With the freedom to raise our families as we please. And the oh-so-precious freedom to worship without fear of retribution.

We've lived in a land where education is a given. Where financial opportunities have abounded. We've had so many blessings, we could never count them all. And every one of them has come from the gracious hand of God.

But, friends, we've turned our backs on the God who's been so good to us. We've neglected to tell this generation about Him or to instill character and values in their hearts and lives.

We've let sin become the norm and faith become the abnormal. We've allowed others to direct our nation away from the foundations of faith that made us great. We've lost our values. Our moral compass. And some days as I watch the news, I think we've even lost our minds.

This great country of ours has become filled with chaos, hatred, crime, and violence.

Fellow Americans, it's time for us to take an abrupt U-turn. To get on our knees, fall on our faces, and beg God to have mercy on us as we reclaim this amazing country of ours for Him.

Where are the righteous men, women, and children who will take a stand for God? Who will fight for our beloved nation? Will you be one of them? Because it sure would be heartbreaking to see God remove His hand of blessing from America.

Yankee Doodle

1. When was the last time you stopped long enough to take a good look at how God has blessed America? Take time to do that today.
2. Psalm 33:12a says, “Blessed is the nation whose God is the LORD” (KJV). But our nation has turned its back on Him. How do you think that will impact His blessings on us?
3. When was the last occasion you spent some real time in God’s Word and in prayer? When was the last time you asked Him to start a revival in you, personally?
4. What can *you* do to make a difference in our country? Ask God. He will show you.

Patriot Prayer

Father,

You are the One who made America great. You have showered this great land with Your abundant blessings. Those who came before us were faithful to serve You. To plant those seeds of faith in our generation. As we look at the state of our country and our world as it is today, turning our country around sometimes seems impossible—but You are the God of the impossible. Start a revival in us. Give us a contagious faith. Give us boldness to share about You with others—because our nation has never needed You more. And, God, please keep Your hand of blessing on this land we love so much.

Amen.

We often think that just one person can't do much, but one woman—an atheist—took a stand to get Bible reading and prayer out of our public schools. Just one woman. But her actions had a profound impact. God used one little boy with five smooth stones to take down the giant, Goliath. Just one little boy. Fellow patriot, today is the day to take a stand for God and our country—even if you're the only one. But you won't be. Because there are many more of us who have decided to take that stand for this land we love, to make sure that we will continue to be a nation whose God is the Lord—so His blessings will always be on America.

CHAPTER THREE

The Other Side

"But I say unto you, Love your enemies, bless them that curse you, do good to them that hate you, and pray for them which despitefully use you, and persecute you."
—Matthew 5:44 (KJV)

Those from "the other side" often give us lots of reasons to talk about them and what they're doing, don't they? They're taking our country in a direction we don't want, and sometimes—to be completely honest—they're ugly and vicious with their comments. It's difficult to like someone like that, isn't it?

Guess what, friends? If we take a good look at ourselves, and are honest about what we see, there have probably been occasions when we've been less than kind with our comments about *their* actions and viewpoints.

But God commands us to love them. To bless them. To do good to them. And to pray for them. Yes, even for those who hate us and our Christian values. Even for those people whose strident voices rake across our last good nerve as they seek to destroy everything we believe, everything precious to us. But when was the last time we've prayed for them? Have we ever done that?

What if we prayed for them as much as we've talked about them and their actions? What if we showed kindness to them so they could see Christ in us? What if we asked

God to help us see them as He sees them? What if we loved them like He loves us—despite our flaws and failures?

We don't have to back down a bit from what we believe. We can still stand strong for our faith and for the values upon which this great country was founded. But maybe if we did what this verse commands us to do, God could work in their hearts.

Before he met Jesus, my pastor, Keith, was a wild young man. He did many things that cause him to feel shame and regret today. But get this! Even though he was out of high school, nobody had ever invited him to church. Nobody. Until the girl he was dating did. He refused, but she kept asking.

His girlfriend, Tina, lived with her grandparents. Keith worked second shift and one night, he arrived at their house after she had gone to bed. Her papaw invited him in and asked, "Do you like peanut butter and jelly? I'll make us some sandwiches."

That night, as Keith left, that godly papaw said, "Keith, I'm praying for you and I love you." Those words and Papaw's kindness and love softened that young man's heart so the gospel could touch him and turn his life around.

Friends, maybe it's time to reach the other side with some prayer, peanut butter, and Papaw.

Yankee Doodle

1. Why do you think God gave us these instructions in today's verse?
2. Take time for an honest look at your heart. Have you been doing what He's asked you to do in this verse?
3. Why do love, kindness, and prayer make such a big difference—in others as well as in you?
4. How do you think the wisdom in this verse could impact our culture?

Patriot Prayer

Father,

It's difficult to love those who we feel are trying to destroy our country—especially if they've been vicious in their attacks on us and our values. But You command us to love them, to pray for them, to bless them, and to do good to them. I'll try, but I know I'll need your help to do that. Help me to remember that nobody might have ever told them about You—and that I might be the only one who will. Help me to see them as You see them. Let them see You in me. Soften their hearts, Lord, and soften mine. Give them a desire to find You. Make me faithful to pray for them.

Amen.

Think of five people from the other side who need your prayers. These can be elected officials, members of the news media, or even vocal members in organizations or the entertainment industry. We've all talked about what they're doing to destroy our country, but talking to Jesus about them will be far more beneficial. Ask ten of your friends to do the same. Then, ask each of them to ask ten of their friends. Let's start some contagious faith. Fellow patriots, here's a sober thought: you might be the only person who's ever prayed for them— or ever will.

CHAPTER FOUR

MORNING GLORY

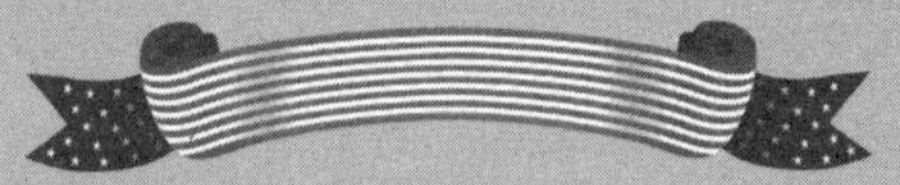

"From the rising of the sun unto the going down of the same the Lord's name is to be praised."
—Psalm 113:3 (KJV)

As dawn breaks over the eastern seaboard and the morning sun begins to spill its light across the waters of the Atlantic, there stands a monument of marble and granite rising high above our nation's capital.

The beacon rises to more than 555 feet and provides a perfect panoramic of the sixty-nine square miles that comprise the District of Columbia. To the north is the White House; to the south, the Jefferson Memorial; to the west, the Lincoln Memorial; and to the east, the Capitol. But no building is as tall as the obelisk.

At its pinnacle is a capstone made of aluminum. It was the intention of her architect, Robert Mills, to carve tributes on all four sides of the capstone—but it's the message he carved on the eastern side of the monument which holds the most importance.

The words have weathered time and turmoil, war and peace. To this day, the seven letters Mr. Mills carved into the aluminum capstone remain.

Laus Deo.

And when morning comes to America, the first rays of light illuminate the capstone—and Mr. Mill's testimony for the ages. You see, the obelisk may celebrate a man, but it gives glory to a higher power—Laus Deo—praise be to God.

I think about the Washington Monument whenever I hear historians debating whether or not our nation was meant to be founded as a Christian nation.

For what it's worth, John Adams, the second president of the United States, was pretty clear which of the "gods" to thank.

In a letter to his wife, Abigail, on the day the Declaration of Independence was approved by Congress, he wrote that July 4th "ought to be commemorated, as the Day of Deliverance by Solemn Acts of Devotion to God Almighty."

Consider the words of former President Ronald Reagan who once said our Founding Fathers believed faith in God was the key to our being a good people and a great nation. "I also believe this blessed land was set apart in a very special way, a country created by men and women who came here not in search of gold, but in search of God." He continued, "They would be free people, living under the law with faith in their Maker and their future. Sometimes, it seems we've strayed from that noble beginning, from our conviction that standards of right and wrong do exist and must be lived up to."

Not a Christian nation? Tell that to the men who wrote our Declaration of Independence. The Preamble states: "We hold these truths to be self-evident, that all men are created equal, that they are endowed by their Creator with certain unalienable Rights, that among these are Life, Liberty and the pursuit of Happiness."

Not a Christian nation? Tell that to George Washington. He used fifty-four biblical terms to describe God in his various writings.

"While we are zealously performing the duties of good Citizens and soldiers we certainly ought not to be inattentive to the higher duties of Religion—To the distinguished Character of Patriot, it should be our highest Glory to add the more distinguished Character of Christian," he once wrote.

Not a Christian nation? Tell that to John Jay, the first Chief Justice of the Supreme Court. "Providence has given to our people the choice of their rulers, and it is the duty, as well as the privilege and interest of our Christian nation to select and prefer Christians for their rulers," he wrote in a letter to Jedidiah Morse in 1797.

Not a Christian nation? Tell that to James Madison, our fourth president and a signer of the US Constitution. In a letter to William Bradford in 1772, he wrote, "Nevertheless, a watchful eye must be kept on ourselves lest while we are building ideal monuments of Renown and

Bliss here we neglect to have our names enrolled in the Annals of Heaven."

Secular humanists may one day be successful in the religious cleansing of American history. But while the winds of change may sweep across the nation's capital—there stands a beacon of hope—a reminder that this nation of immigrants was built, not on sinking sand, but on a firm foundation, girded by Almighty God. And unless someone has a really tall ladder—and a blow torch, the first rays of morning light will shine down upon these United States of America—illuminating an eternal truth and a grateful nation's prayer—praise be to God!

Laus Deo.

Yankee Doodle

1. How do we know that our forefathers intended for our country to be established on Christian principles?
2. How are the words "Laus Deo" part of Robert Mill's testimony—and why should they be part of ours?
3. President Ronald Reagan believed that our faith was an important key to us being a great nation. How do you think our nation moving away from God has impacted us?
4. Why is it crucial for our nation to have Christian leaders?

Patriot Prayer

Father,

Our country was established on Christian principles. For numerous generations, those principles were protected and valued, but our generation has neglected to protect those values. We've stood by silently as our religious freedoms have been trampled upon. Lord, give us the character and the courage of those who've come before us. Help us to take a stand for You and our nation. Help us to remember that our faith is vital for America to be great. Praise be to You for blessing our country as You have for so many generations. Help us to pass down those values to the generations to come so that our beloved country will always be one nation under God.

Amen.

Much of our country's history has been removed from our textbooks, and our children are not being taught those lessons and stories about how our country was established on faith and Christian principles. Buy old textbooks for your children and grandchildren so they'll know what truly happened in the past. Take time to teach them about the men and women who made our country the grandest on earth, and how faith was such a big part of that. We can't afford to forget where we've come from.

Sweet Potato Biscuits with Honey-Glazed Ham

From the Kitchen of Aunt Rainey (Lorraine Sherlin)

Ingredients:

- 3 cups canned sweet potatoes
- 3 packages active dry yeast
- ¾ cup warm water (105 to 115 degrees)
- 7 ½ cups all-purpose flour
- 1 tablespoon baking powder
- 1 tablespoon salt
- 1 ½ cups sugar
- 1 ½ cups shortening
- Slices of honey-glazed ham

Directions:

Drain the sweet potatoes and then mash them; set aside. Mix the yeast and warm water together and then let it sit for five minutes. While the yeast is blooming, combine the all-purpose flour, baking powder, salt, and sugar. Cut in the shortening with a pastry blender, a fork, or two table knives held side by side until the mixture is crumbly. Add the yeast mixture and the mashed sweet potatoes. Stir until all the dry ingredients are moistened.

Once everything is combined well, turn the dough out on a lightly-floured surface. Knead the dough for five minutes, then place in a lightly-greased bowl, turning the biscuit dough to grease the top. Cover the dough and put it in the refrigerator overnight (or for at least eight hours).

Roll the dough on a lightly-floured surface to ½” thickness. Cut with a 2” round biscuit cutter. Place the biscuits on ungreased baking sheets. Cover the baking sheets and let the cut biscuits rise in a warm place that’s free from drafts. This should take about 30 minutes or until they’re almost doubled in bulk. Bake at 400 degrees for about 10 to 12 minutes or until the biscuits are lightly browned.

Serve with honey-glazed ham.

*Unbaked biscuits can be frozen for up to a month. When ready to use, remove the biscuits from the freezer and let the dough thaw for 30 minutes, then cover the baking sheet and let rise in a warm place that's free from drafts for about 30 minutes or until they're almost doubled in bulk. Bake as directed.

CHAPTER FIVE

The Things We've Taken for Granted

"But the hour is coming, and now is,
when the true worshipers will worship the Father
in spirit and truth; for the Father is seeking such
to worship Him."
—John 4:23 (NKJV)

Have you ever stopped to think about what a precious gift it is to go to church, own a Bible, and worship openly? It's something we really need to think about, because those freedoms are under attack, and we're seeing open hostility toward people of faith.

Friends, there are folks all over the world who would give anything for those freedoms which we've taken for granted. There are countries where people have to hide to worship—where they can go to prison for gathering to hear about God, or where their lives are at stake if they're discovered. Can you imagine the courage that must take and the anxiety they must feel in those moments as they meet together? But it's worth it to them.

How many times have we sat in church and taken it for granted because we gather on Sunday morning, Sunday evening, and Wednesday nights for services—just like we always have.

There are countries where simply *owning* a Bible can cost folks their freedom or even their lives. Places where people would give anything to hold a copy of God's Word in their hands. Where they gratefully receive scraps of paper with handwritten verses of Scripture so they can memorize them and then destroy those pages before they're discovered.

A missionary told a story about being in a country where there were harsh punishments for having church services. He shared about a man whose legs had been amputated to above the knees. That man heard that there would be a church service in the neighboring town, and for hours in the hot sun and the blistering sand, he laboriously scooted his way to church.

That man knew what a precious gift it was to gather with others to hear about Jesus. Tears dripped down my cheeks as I thought about how seldom I'd thanked God for the priceless gift of driving to church, being with fellow believers, singing songs of worship, and hearing a sermon that either convicted or blessed me. Like most of us, I'd taken it for granted.

But we no longer have that luxury. Our world, our media, and our country are making a mockery of our faith. They're attempting to silence us. Bible studies, gathering at homes to worship together, and even religious events and holidays such as Christmas and Easter have come under attack.

Jesus loves us so much that He died for us. Will we love Him enough to become warriors of faith? To fight for our religious liberties? To say, "Enough is enough!" and to take a stand for Him? We must.

1. How long has it been since you thought about our priceless gift of religious freedom—and thanked God for that? Do it today.
2. Hold your Bible in your hands. Take time to thank God for it. Pray for those who would give anything to own a Bible. And then pray for those who've never heard about God's amazing love.
3. Next time you go to church, thank God for the privilege of being able to worship Him freely and openly. Then, pray for those who can't.
4. What can you do to help preserve our religious freedom for another generation? Ask God to give you courage and boldness.

Patriot Prayer

Father,

My heart breaks as I look at the state of our country, as I see how our religious freedoms are under attack. Those who came before us protected that freedom of faith and handed it down to us. Help us to be just as faithful. Lord, make us warriors who will say, "I'm not going to sit back and do nothing!" Make us as faithful and determined as that sweet man who scooted to church. Have mercy on us. I know we don't deserve it, but for the sake of the next generations, we beg You for it. Help us to speak up when needed. To get on our knees with tears on our cheeks as we pray for America. Turn our nation back to You.

Amen.

Evil flourishes when we do nothing. Talk to your schools and elected officials if your child's rights to mention God are violated. Take a stand for things that happen in your neighborhood or community that are against religious freedom. Speak out on social media when you see things that make a mockery of God and our faith. Your efforts will inspire someone else. Pray for America as you've never prayed before. Not just a simple, "Bless America, God." Pray from your heart, with tears dripping down your face. Because if we don't pray earnestly for America, who will?

CHAPTER SIX

The Power of One

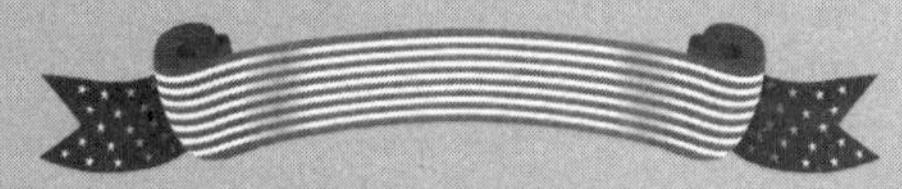

"O Lord, I pray, please let Your ear be attentive to the prayer of Your servant, and to the prayer of Your servants who desire to fear Your name; and let Your servant prosper this day."
—Nehemiah 1:11a (NKJV)

A recent video shared the moment when an announcer came over the loudspeaker and said to play ball—and that there would be no rendition of the national anthem that day. There was silence for a moment, and then one voice began singing, and then another, and another, until the glorious sound of "The Star-Spangled Banner" echoed throughout the ballpark as everyone stood to their feet and sang.

Friends, that's the power of one. One citizen who said, "We *are* going to sing our national anthem." One person who stood with righteous indignation and declared, "We *are* going to respect and honor our country."

In the Bible, a man named Nehemiah—the king's cupbearer—became concerned about Jerusalem. When he heard how broken his beloved country was, he mourned, wept, fasted, and prayed.

The king noticed his sad demeanor and asked what was wrong. Nehemiah prayed once more and became bold, asking if he could go to rebuild his country, if the king would write letters to smooth the way, and if he'd provide the lumber they would need.

He was just one man with a burden for his country.

Nehemiah went to Jerusalem and took stock of the situation there. What he saw broke his heart. Then, he asked the Jews, the priests, the nobles, the rulers, and others to help him rebuild the city and the walls around it. This is where the power of one became the power of many, as person after person and group after group said, "I'll do this part!" and others took another task, and so on.

It wasn't easy. They were mocked. People tried to block their efforts. (Doesn't that sound familiar, fellow patriots?) But one man—Nehemiah—stood strong with righteous indignation for his city. As he told his people in Nehemiah 4:20b (KJV), "...Our God shall fight for us."

The story of Nehemiah went from being one man with a burden for his country, to thousands of people who gathered together to build the wall to secure Jerusalem from attacks. They worked with fervor, for the task of rebuilding their country was too important for them to be sidetracked.

They identified sin and wrongdoing—the areas where they'd moved away from God—and removed those things from their city. And they worshipped. They knew the source of their strength.

Because of the power of one man who became burdened for his country—one man armed with the power of God—things changed.

Tears mist my eyes today as I write this. Do it again, Lord, for America. Do it again!

YANKEE DOODLE

1. When someone made a decision to no longer play the national anthem at that ballgame, everyday citizens became involved. That's you, friends. What can *you* do to become involved in the process of rebuilding our country?
2. How long has it been since you took a really good look at our country? Take time today to make a list of the things that concern you, of the ways our country is moving toward destruction.
3. When's the last time you've wept and mourned for America? That you've fasted and prayed for our country? Ask God to give you a burden for this great land of ours.
4. What happened after Nehemiah got a burden for Jerusalem?

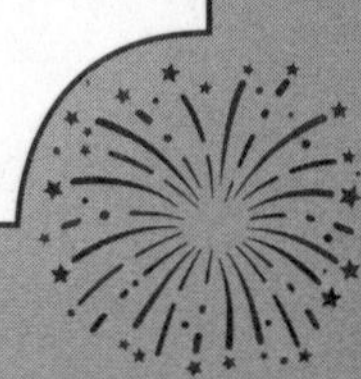

Patriot Prayer

Father,

I want to be like those people at that ballgame, to have the courage of my convictions where I will take a stand for what's right. I want to have the heart of Nehemiah, so that when I take a good look at my country, I will cry for it, I will mourn for how we've moved away from the God who made us great, and I will bombard Heaven for healing for our land. Where I will say, "I MUST do something." Where I'll say, "God, what will You have me do?" Where I'll be filled with such righteous indignation that I will work with all my might to make a difference. Father, heal this land that I love so much.

Amen.

Fellow patriots, the power of one is amazing, but when we gather together and harness the power of thousands and millions of likeminded people, we become a force that can't be stopped. What can you do? Pray! Share your faith. Volunteer during the election season to help get the vote out for candidates who share your values. Research the candidates. Get others involved. Speak up for what you believe. And be willing to take a stand even if nobody else will. God will honor that.

CHAPTER SEVEN

HEROES

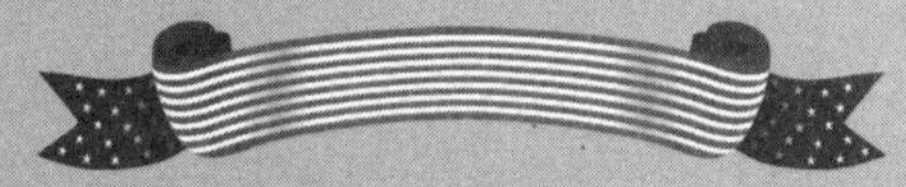

"And the angel of the Lord appeared to him and said to him, 'The Lord is with you, valiant warrior.'"

—Judges 6:12 (NASB)

I treasure a photo from World War II of my dad and his brothers in their Navy uniforms. Whenever I look at that black-and-white image, I always think about the worry my grandmother must have felt as four of her sons sailed off to fight for our country in dangerous areas of the world.

Many times on the news, I've watched the remains of fallen soldiers returned to American soil. Even though I didn't know any of them, my eyes would fill with tears as those flag-covered coffins were solemnly removed from the planes flying them home to their brokenhearted families. Their sacrifice meant something.

But it became personal the day I received word that a friend's son had been killed when his helicopter was shot down during Desert Storm. This handsome young man had signed up for a second tour of duty because he looked into the sweet faces of his nieces and nephews and knew that he *must* return to the battlefield so they would have a free and safe country. He willingly gave his life for them and America.

During my years in politics, I worked with a man who'd been a POW for almost eight years. He told me how he and his fellow soldiers ate rats because they were so hungry. I was in his office several months later, and he mentioned that it was the birthday of one of the communist leaders from that country. I asked him why he knew that, and he replied, "They starved us for months before that day, and then on his birthday, they'd give us an extra ration of rice." My heart broke as I imagined the horror those men had endured. Those heroes—and their families at home—paid a great price for the freedoms we so often take for granted.

There's one other hero I must mention as well—a Savior who loves us all so much that He willingly gave His life so that we may be forgiven from our sins, and so we can live with the freedom of salvation. And because of that sacrifice, we have hope.

Dear ones, we have a solemn responsibility to God and to those who've fought for our country. We must become heroes of faith, willing to fight to preserve our religious freedoms. To make America God's again. To protect the principles that made our country great.

As we look at our nation, this seems like an insurmountable task. But as our verse today reminds us, we don't need to be afraid and we don't need to worry, because the Lord will be with us.

Yankee Doodle

1. Stop and think about the sacrifices that have been made to protect this amazing country and our freedoms. How have you benefited from what those heroes did?
2. Stop and think about the precious sacrifice Jesus made so that we can be forgiven and free from our sins. How has that impacted your life?
3. What sacrifices are you willing to make to fight for our country and our religious freedoms—and to protect those for another generation?
4. Even though our nation has been in such a big mess, why don't we need to worry or be afraid?

Patriot Prayer

Father,

I'm so grateful for all those heroes who have fought for our country—and even given their lives so that we can be free. We can't afford to let their sacrifice be in vain. Our ancestors were faithful to preserve and protect our faith and our values so that our generation can enjoy them as well. They found a cause worth fighting for and, because of that, they left us the grandest nation in the world—one where we can worship You freely, and tell others about You. Thank You, Lord, for Your amazing sacrifice that changed the world…and me. Help us to pass that message on to the next generation, and to a thousand generations thereafter.

Amen.

Take a look at the sweet faces of your children, your grandchildren, or another child you love. How can we possibly leave them a world and country where they're not allowed to mention God's name or to share their faith with someone else? We can't. God's looking for a few good men and women who will say, "I'm reporting for duty, Lord. What do You need me to do?" Let's become mighty warriors for God. Let's fight for what is right and just. Let's return America to the God who made her great.

CHAPTER EIGHT

God Bless Whoopie Pie

"Then make my joy complete by being like-minded, having the same love, being one in spirit and of one mind."
—Philippians 2:2 (NIV)

Covering presidential campaigns was one of my favorite assignments during my time at Fox News. It provided me a front-row seat to history and a chance to understand the men who wanted to lead our nation. More often than not, my colleagues in the media would declare that the United States was a divided nation. I was a bit circumspect of their analysis, so I decided to set off on a journey across the country to see if, in fact, we were a nation that pitted brother against brother.

My search for answers took me through the cornfields of Iowa and the waters of South Carolina's low country; I traversed the Mississippi Delta and braved the scorching heat of the Nevada deserts. I was nearly mugged in Detroit and caught the flu in Chicago, but I pressed on toward the prize. And one day, it suddenly hit me. I was somewhere between a red state and a blue state when I had something of a political epiphany.

It happened at a small diner tucked away on a side street in the picturesque town of Manchester, New Hampshire. The Red Arrow Diner has been serving up blue-plate specials on Lowell Street since 1922. And it's also become a mandatory stop on the campaign trail for anyone who wants to take up residence at 1600 Pennsylvania Avenue.

It was a cold, snowy day, just before the New Hampshire primary. I peeled off my winter coat and grabbed the first stool I could find. The waitress told me they made the best meatloaf in town so that's what I ordered—along with a root beer.

As I was waiting for my meal, I thought about my epiphany. I found a nation with a lot more in common than the network news agencies would admit.

Most folks across the fruited plain really are alike. We work hard, tend backyard gardens, go to high school football games on Friday nights, and go to church on Sundays. In a way, that's what makes our country so wonderful—and the fabric of our freedom so strong.

Consider our fellow countrymen in New Hampshire. They understand the cost of freedom. It's emblazoned on every car in the state: "Live Free or Die." As soon as I crossed the state line from Massachusetts, I found a Cracker Barrel restaurant, picked up a country music station on the radio, and came across a NASCAR racetrack. For a minute, I thought I made a wrong turn and ended up in Alabama.

In between bites of meatloaf at the Red Arrow Diner, I contemplated the American narrative, wondering why God chose to shed His grace on this land, on this people.

Maybe it has something to do with the fact that a small, but determined group of pilgrims sacrificed everything to come to this land so that they could worship God without the fear of being persecuted.

Maybe it has something to do with the nature of our people—that volunteer spirit—where neighbors help neighbors. Maybe it has something to do with the notion that we are a free people because our freedom is rooted in our faith.

I'm able to write these very words because I am free. We can go to church on Sunday because we are free. We gather in courthouse squares and protest the government because we are free.

Sometimes I wonder if we've forgotten about this most unique and wonderful gift God has given us. We read the newspapers and magazines and learn America is supposedly in decline—that it is a country that has lost its footing on the international stage.

We've seen presidents stand on foreign soil and apologize on our behalf. Well, quite frankly, who cares what the French or Russians think about us?

I'm reminded of the words of Commodore Stephen Decatur: "Our country! In her intercourse with foreign nations may she always be in the right; but our country, right or wrong."

They call us bitter Americans—people who love this country unconditionally, people who pledge allegiance to the flag, people who believe in God, people who go to church, people who volunteer to take up arms and defend our nation against evil, people who believe marriage is a covenant before God between a man and a woman.

Meanwhile, back inside the Red Arrow Diner, I was polishing off the last bites of the meatloaf when the waitress suggested I try some dessert.

"Sure. How about some sweet potato pie?"

"Honey, that's a Southern dessert. You're in New Hampshire."

"What would you suggest?"

"How about some whoopie?" she asked, matter-of-factly.

"Excuse me?" I asked, turning beet red.

"Whoopie. Would you like some whoopie?"

"I'm flattered," I said. "But we've just met—and I'm a Baptist."

The waitress gave me a distressed look and then whacked me on the head with a menu. "It's a pie," she said. "Whoopie pie."

I ordered the pie—with an extra dollop of whipped cream. And it was good.

As I sipped on a cup of coffee, I was reminded of the lyrics from that great Lee Greenwood song. Words that remind us to take pride in being an American. To celebrate our freedom. To be willing to take a stand to defend our country. And for God to bless this land we love so much.

May God bless America and may He also bless whoopie pie.

Yankee Doodle

1. Why do you think God chose to shed His grace on our nation?
2. The pilgrims came to America so they could worship God without fear of persecution. How has that impacted you?
3. Our freedom is rooted in our faith. Why is it important for you to remember that?
4. We often forget about God's blessings to us. When's the last time you thanked God for the privilege of being an American and for the rights such a privilege gives you?

Patriot Prayer

Father,

Thank You for those brave pilgrims who took a stand and traveled to America so they could worship You without fear of being persecuted. Because of their courage, I have been blessed. Help me to never take my freedoms for granted. Help me to remember that my freedom is rooted in my faith—and that when my faith falters, my nation will as well. Thank You for shedding Your grace on our beloved country. We don't deserve it, but we are so thankful. Thank You for the precious privilege of being an American and for the rights and freedoms that I have because of that. You have blessed me and our country and I am so grateful.

Amen.

Take some time today and study about the pilgrims. Why do you think it was so important for them to be able to worship God without fear of persecution? What had they experienced before they arrived in America? What gave them the courage to do something as drastic as leaving their homeland? Why is religious freedom so vital, and what religious rights have you seen slip away or be threatened in recent history? It's important for us to never forget where we've come from as a country.

Todd's Favorite Meatloaf

From the Kitchen of Michelle Cox

Ingredients:

3 pounds ground chuck
½ cup chopped onion (I use Vidalia or other sweet onions)
1 egg
¾ cup evaporated milk
½ cup quick oats
1 ¼ teaspoons salt
1 ½ cups cheddar cheese

Topping:

2/3 cup ketchup
½ cup packed brown sugar
1 ½ teaspoon yellow mustard

Directions:

Mix together all ingredients (except for the topping ones). Place into a 13x9x2 casserole dish that has been sprayed with cooking spray, shaping the meatloaf mixture into a football-like shape, just not as tall.

Bake uncovered at 350 degrees for about 30 minutes. Drain off the grease. Mix the topping ingredients and spread over the meatloaf. Bake for an additional 20–25 minutes.

*This meatloaf bakes completely in my oven at this amount of time. Todd's found it takes a little longer in his oven. Since all ovens can cook things a little differently, bake until there's no pink in the center and it's completely done.

**If I have leftover meatloaf, I slice it and then freeze it in single-serving or two-serving sizes. I love having things in the freezer that I can pull out and heat up for a quick meal on extra busy days. I just reheat the slices in the microwave.

Note: Paul and I love it when Todd comes to stay with us for a few days. On one of Todd's visits, I fixed this meatloaf and served it with twice-baked-potato casserole and coleslaw. Todd took the recipe home and has made it multiple times since then.

Our youngest son is a full-time youth pastor. Each winter and summer, he plans a youth camp week for the teens at our church. They love it. They have tons of fun, but they also have services to deepen their faith and character. This year's summer camp happened just recently, and it wasn't too far from our house, so we drove across the mountain to join them for one of the evening services. It was a sweet time, and came with a message the teens needed.

Five of our grandchildren were there, and at the end of the evening, we made our rounds, hugging all of them goodbye and telling them we love them. As I reached to hug our oldest granddaughter, she clasped me in a tight hug. I could tell she was emotional from the way she clung to me.

And then, in a voice laden with tears, she softly said, "Grandmama, thank you for teaching my daddy how to serve God so he could teach me." I can't tell you how those words hit my heart. Tears still well up every time I think about it, and I will cherish that moment for the rest of my life.

CHAPTER NINE

FROM GENERATION TO GENERATION

"Tell your children about it,
let your children tell their children,
and their children another generation."
—Joel 1:3 (NKJV)

Friends, every minute you spend teaching your children and grandchildren about God is worth it. All those days when you taught them Bible verses and songs about Jesus? When you told them Bible stories? When you taught them about character and values and to love and respect others and our country? Keep doing it, because there's no greater joy than seeing your children grow up and serve God—and our country has never needed that more.

All those late-night drives to the church to pick them up from youth activities? They were an investment. Those countless hours you spent on your knees praying for a rebellious child or a prodigal one? They were worth it—even if you haven't yet seen the results.

I'm grateful for a precious grandpa who didn't just talk about Jesus, but lived for Him every day. His love for God's Word inspired me. His sweetness of spirit touched me. And his example of what it meant to be a *real* Christian impacted my life.

I can go back through our family tree on both my side and my husband's and find person after person who lived faithfully for God, who passed down their faith to the next generation and to their community.

But I don't just want to look back, I want to look forward and see that our legacy of faith is being handed down to future generations. Because that's what will make America truly great again.

1. Life is busy and hard. Sometimes you're tired and it's tempting to just let your family stay home from church or to skip family devotions. Why is it so important for you to show an example of faithfulness to your children and grandchildren?
2. What values and character traits do you most want to instill in your children and grandchildren?
3. How often do you pray for your family? If you don't do it, who will?
4. How can building a strong family of faith impact our nation?

Patriot Prayer

Father,

Thank You for those who taught me about You so that I could teach my sons—and so they can teach my grandchildren how to serve You. More than anything, I want that faith to carry on through countless generations. It's vital that our nation repent and turn back to You and the principles that made America great. There are so many people who seek to send our children in another direction, and I know I must remain vigilant about planting those seeds of faith in their hearts. God, I pray for my family. Help us to serve You faithfully and to finish well. Give us all boldness to always take a stand for You.

Amen.

Our schools, social media, music, television, and movies are full of anti-Christian values, and our country has many people and organizations with an agenda to take over the minds and hearts of our children. Protect the eyes and ears of your children and teens. Know what they watch. Know what's going on at their schools. Know what they're doing on social media. Pay attention to who they're hanging out with. Be diligent about teaching them your values and about God—because if you don't, someone else will implant *their* values and disdain for God in your children and grandchildren.

CHAPTER TEN

Land That I Love

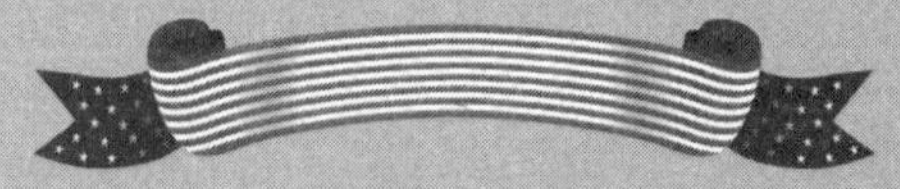

"Blessed is the nation whose God is the LORD."
—Psalm 33:12a (KJV)

I'll never forget the moment many years ago when, along with my fellow delegates to the Republican National Convention, we stood to our feet with thousands of others in the convention hall and sang along with Lee Greenwood as he belted out "God Bless the USA." The moment was electrifying as American pride unfurled, folks waved flags, and we celebrated being Americans.

I love this nation with which God's blessed us. I still smile when I drive down a country road and see the American flag on a mailbox or hanging from the porch of an old farmhouse. I feel pride when I pass by a business with a giant American flag flying in the breeze with a cloudless blue sky for a background. It is such a thing of beauty.

I feel safety and security when I've been in another country, and I come back through the airport and see the sign that I'm back on American soil again.

I love Fourth of July celebrations with family and friends dressed in red, white, and blue as we honor our country. With the aroma of hot dogs and hamburgers on the grill. With fresh corn on the cob, tomatoes, and watermelons shared from backyard gardens.

I look forward to church dinners on the grounds, tables piled high with fried chicken, potato salad, banana pudding, and dozens of other delights. Opportunities for fellowship with other believers. And the hymn singing that follows those dinners, carrying sweet harmonies that ring out with the precious promises of those old songs.

And I love it when I drive through a community and hear the unexpected sound of church bells. Oh, how we need to hear more of that clanging throughout our nation!

I experience awe as I travel across this vast land of ours and experience the wonder of God's amazing creation. From the blue-ridged mountains of North Carolina, to the sugar-white sands and turquoise waters of Florida; through the cotton fields of Alabama to the swamps of Louisiana. From the oil fields and ranch land of Texas and Oklahoma, to the Rocky Mountains of Colorado and the redwood forests of California.

From the majesty of the Tetons and the buffalo still roaming the fields of Montana, and the towering arched red rocks of Utah, to the cornfields of Indiana, the music-filled hills of Tennessee, and the autumn splendor of Vermont. All of it is designed by a God who loves us and enjoys giving us pleasure. It's no wonder we're known as America the beautiful—and it's no wonder that *this* is the land that I love.

Yankee Doodle

1. What do you love about our country? Take time to thank God for America today. Share those thoughts with your children and grandchildren.
2. How has God blessed our nation? What things make you proud to be an American?
3. Why do moments of patriotism and faith move you to emotion?
4. Why are the old hymns still relevant in our lives today?

Patriot Prayer

Father,

America is beautiful beyond words. Photos don't do it justice when we try to capture what we see. You're an awe-inspiring God, and the work of Your hands is stunning. Even if we're not wealthy, we are rich because of all the ways that You have blessed our beloved nation. Help me to never take those blessings for granted, and to remember that to whom much is given, much is required. Help us to be faithful caretakers of our great country. Of the beauty. Of the faith. And of the principles and values upon which this great land of ours was established. Thank You for all Your blessings on America, and on us.

Amen.

Sometimes we need to look at our lives with fresh eyes. To take stock of all the blessings we've received. To make time to tour our country. Start with your town, and then move on to other cities in your state. As funds allow, branch out to other parts of our nation. Enjoy the beauty. Learn about the history of those areas. Visit the churches and worship with other Americans. Take pictures. Make memories. And tell your children and grandchildren all of these things are because we're a nation that has been deeply blessed by God.

CHAPTER ELEVEN

What Are We Leaving Behind?

"For I have chosen him, so that he will direct his children and his household after him to keep the way of the Lord by doing what is right and just."
—Genesis 18:19a (NIV)

All of us want to leave behind a legacy for our loved ones. It's wonderful to leave them financial blessings, but there are even more important goals we need to think about. What kind of country are we leaving behind? Will future generations have the same freedoms we've known as Americans? Will they be able to attend the church of their choice, worship freely, and speak openly about their faith?

It's not looking good unless we the people return to God and pray for Him to have mercy on America. Unless we take a stand for what's right—just as fervently as those who wish to destroy our values.

I can drive around my town and the neighboring one and find visible proof that those who came before us were faithful to do those things. Mine and my husband's ancestors were involved in starting and building numerous churches throughout our area. It gives me great joy whenever I drive by one of them that is still active and think of those long-ago family members who saw a need and did something about it.

After the Civil War, one of my (however many great) grandfathers returned home from his position as chief chaplain for the troops. I'm sure his heart was heavy from all he'd seen and from the state of the country.

He and a friend saw a need for a church in their community. They prayed. They donated their own money, got people enthused to help, and raised other funds until they had enough to start building. Soon, the sound of hymns and sermons echoed out of the windows and doors as folks passed by. For more than 130 years, that church was active in our city, touching hearts and changing lives with the gospel.

But you know what's sad to me? A recent newspaper article shared that this church was closing their doors for the last time. Now, if you dial their phone number, you get a recording saying it's no longer in service. At a time when our society has never needed the impact of churches more, many of them are closing as their congregations dwindle or their elderly attendees die off.

Friends, we have the best news in all the world—but sometimes we treat it like it's a well-kept secret. It's time for us to start sharing it. The answers to fix our nation are all in God's Word, and it's time for us to put that wisdom into action. Because it's not acceptable for our faith to no longer be in service.

1. Are you happy with the legacy we're leaving behind as a country? As people of faith?
2. How do you feel when you learn a church has closed their doors? How does that impact our society?
3. Why are all of us sometimes so hesitant about sharing our faith? What if nobody had ever shared Jesus with you?
4. What are some answers from the Bible that would help to guide our culture in the right direction?

Patriot Prayer

Father,

As I've seen churches and Christian bookstores close their doors, it's made me sad. Our light of faith is growing dim in many communities, and yet, we've never needed our lights to shine brightly more than we do now. Help others to see Jesus in us and to want what we have. Even though it's sometimes out of my comfort zone to witness to people, give me a boldness to share what You've done for me, and what You can do for them. Help us to leave behind a strong legacy of faith for those who will come after us.

Amen.

Friends, people need what we have. If it's hard for you to share your faith, here are a few suggestions. Leave a gospel tract when you go out to eat, are on public transportation, or anywhere else you can find. You might think that doesn't have a big impact, but I know of a woman who was on a subway one day. She was ready to commit suicide when she got off, but instead, she found a gospel tract, read it, asked Jesus to save her, and went on to live an amazing life for God. Another idea is to purchase some New Testaments and Bibles at dollar stores. Hand the New Testaments out to homeless people and others God leads you to. When you travel, if there's not a Bible in your room, leave one in a drawer. Even wearing shirts with Christian messages can help to share about Jesus.

CHAPTER TWELVE

No Greater Love

"Greater love hath no man than this,
that a man lay down his life for his friends."
—John 15:13 (KJV)

Navy veteran Jerry Wayne Pino died on December 12th in Long Beach, Mississippi. He was seventy years old.

We don't know that much about Jerry. He was born in Baton Rouge and joined the Navy in New Orleans. He was a Petty officer third class in Vietnam. That's the extent of his biography.

No family. No friends. He died alone.

Jerry's body lay unclaimed for several weeks at Riemann Family Funeral Homes.

"No one stepped forward," funeral home worker Cathy Warden told me. "He just didn't have any family."

Miss Cathy explained the situation to her colleague, Eva Boomer, and together they decided something must be done to give this veteran a proper send-off.

"Something had to be done with respect," Miss Cathy said. "We had to give him what he deserved. Nobody should go alone."

Miss Eva, who is also a veteran, wondered if some of the boys at Long Beach High School might be willing to serve as pallbearers. It was a longshot, though, seeing how most of the students were out on Christmas break.

But Miss Cathy called her teenage son, Bryce who, in turn, texted some of his friends—and within a matter of minutes, six young men had volunteered to serve at a stranger's funeral.

Nobody should go alone.

"It was the right thing to do," seventeen-year-old Bailey Griffin told me. "He served our country. He fought for our rights. For him to be buried with nobody there was just sad. I told myself I was going to do it and I did it."

They buried Petty Officer Third Class Jerry Pino on a Tuesday. The sun was shining and there was a cool, gulf coast breeze meandering through the Biloxi National Cemetery. An honor guard stood at attention.

The boys were smartly dressed in khaki pants and button-down shirts and neck ties. They solemnly took their places on either side of the flag-draped coffin and escorted a man they did not know to his final resting place.

"I went out there for the service and cried the whole way through," Miss Cathy said. "He had no one there. This veteran had nobody standing there but these boys."

But what happened at the end of the funeral was incredibly moving and poignant.

The flag that had draped over Jerry's coffin was folded and presented to the six young men from Long Beach High School, home of the Bearcats.

"It touched my heart," Miss Cathy said.

The *Sun Herald* shared a message from the mother of one of the young pallbearers. "Proud mom when he told me that no one should be buried without people who care present, especially a veteran," Stacie Tripp wrote on Facebook.

"Evidence that moms and dads are doing something right in Long Beach," is what Miss Cathy said. "Our community is teaching these boys from the heart how it should be—how to care."

They are still trying to figure out what to do with the flag that draped Jerry's coffin. It's being encased in glass—along with a plaque that bears his name.

There's talk about putting the flag on display at the high school or perhaps inside the locker room where four of the pallbearers play football.

It would be a fitting tribute to a man who died alone but who was buried surrounded by his fellow countrymen.

What a lesson for the rest of us—demonstrated by a group of young boys from Mississippi who committed in their hearts that nobody should go alone—especially a veteran.

This is a touching story that should inspire each of us as Americans, but it's also a valuable example for us as Christians. Whenever someone is alone, going through a difficult time, or just needs support, we should always be ready to fill that need. As Reverend Ralph Sexton says, "All we have is God and each other."

I think it would please God's heart for us to take some time and look around us. To search for that "forgotten" person amongst us who needs to feel His love and ours. To help that sweet senior citizen who's struggling to make ends meet. To support the single parent who is overwhelmed and could use a helping hand. And to encourage the veteran who needs to hear the words, "Thank you for your service. You're my hero."

Yes, God's love is the greatest love, but we can be the hands and feet to carry that love to others—just like those teen boys did for Navy veteran Jerry Wayne Pino.

Yankee Doodle

1. It's a sad thing to feel lonely or to be alone. What do you think God would have us do to help others in that position?
2. Showing kindness and compassion doesn't cost anything but our time. Why are we sometimes slow to do that?
3. How can we learn to look for the needs around us—even if nobody mentions them?
4. How can we be the hands and feet of Jesus to those who feel forgotten?

Patriot Prayer

Father,

My heart is touched by what those teen boys did for Jerry Wayne Pino. Help me to be the first to step forward whenever there's a need for an individual or my country. Give me a heart of compassion and teach me to look for those who feel forgotten or have nobody to help them. Help me to love like You do. To reach out to others so that everyone feels loved and wanted. To respect and honor those who've served in our military and as first responders. Thank You for a country filled with so many wonderful and caring people. We are blessed.

Amen.

There are people all around us who need somebody to care about them. Let's be intentional about filling those needs. Sit down with your family and come up with a list of five ways you can be a blessing to other people. Perhaps you might want to surprise a widow on a fixed income with a gift card for gas, groceries, or a meal out, along with a note about how much she means to you. Or maybe your entire family might want to bless single parents with a night out while you care for their children, or by helping them clean or do necessary repairs. Find what works for you and become an extension of God's love.

Coconut Cake

From the Kitchen of Michelle Cox

Ingredients:

1 package frozen coconut
1 box yellow cake mix (eggs, oil, and water per pkg. directions)
8 ounces sour cream
2 cups sugar
Medium to large Cool Whip
1 cup flaked coconut

Directions:

Remove the frozen coconut from the freezer to thaw while the cake is baking. Mix the cake together according to the package directions. Spray a 13x9x2 pan with cooking spray, pour the batter into the pan, even it out, and then bake per the package directions. Once the cake is baked, allow it to cool completely, then take the handle of a wooden spoon and poke holes all throughout the cake.

While the cake is cooling, mix the sour cream, sugar, and frozen/thawed coconut together. Spread across the cake, allowing it to fill the holes you've poked into the cake. Frost generously with the Cool Whip, and then sprinkle the cup of flaked coconut over the top. Refrigerate for two days before serving so the flavors will blend and the cake will become moist.

Note: This is easy to make and so delicious! My guests are always delighted when I offer to send some home with them. My son went to a Christmas party for the singles at our church. My sweet friend Teresa Proffitt served this and Tim asked her for the recipe. I've made dozens of coconut cakes since then and it's always a hit.

CHAPTER THIRTEEN

We Can't Be Silent Anymore

"For Zion's sake I will not keep silent,
and for Jerusalem's sake I will not be quiet,
until her righteousness goes forth as brightness,
and her salvation as a burning torch."
—Isaiah 62:1 (ESV)

A friend posted on social media that he'd been rebuked by an old friend for his "ugly comments online." I always read his posts, and I hadn't seen anything even remotely ugly. On the contrary, everything I've ever seen from him has been presented in a kind and loving manner. My friend had simply commented on situations in direct opposition to his values, about things that made a flagrant mockery of his faith.

I've noticed a trend in this direction. Every time a Christian says or posts something taking a stand for what they believe in, others take them to task that they shouldn't say anything because someone might get their feelings hurt.

I'm a firm believer in being Christ-like in how we say or do things, but friends, we can't afford to be silent anymore. That's part of how we've ended up in the mess our country's in right now.

When I was a child, the Ten Commandments were posted in my school. I remember learning Bible verses, and my teachers taught us Bible stories. When they shared about David and Goliath, I learned about faith and courage. When they told the story of Daniel and the lion's den, they taught us about the power of prayer and about being a person of character and commitment even when it might cost us something.

All those lessons taught us to be better people, to be kind, to build character and values, and to be good citizens. But then prayer and Bible reading were taken out of our public schools, and things sure did change after that.

Now, instead of honoring our country, we've watched as people have disrespected our flag by tearing it down, stomping on it, and even setting it on fire. Our national anthem, once sung with pride before ballgames and events, has disappeared from many stadiums.

Things are happening in our country now that would cause our forefathers to roll over in their graves. I can't even imagine their disbelief if they could see the state of America now.

We've allowed sin to creep in (or flood in like the rushing water from a broken dam) and for God to be pushed out of our society. Even many of our pulpits have moved away from powerful sermons based on God's Word to fluffy, feel-good messages.

If we remain silent about the things we value—God and country—we just might see those erased permanently from our society. We need to keep America as "one nation under God."

1. How do you think taking prayer and Bible reading out of our public schools has impacted our country?
2. Have you been one of the silent ones? How can you speak out with kindness when the foundations of our country and our faith are attacked? Why is it so important that you not remain silent anymore?
3. How has America changed since you were a child? What do you miss from those times?
4. What do you see as you look ahead at the country your children and grandchildren will inherit? Are you willing to speak up and take a stand for what's right so that the next generation will have a country as great as what we had?

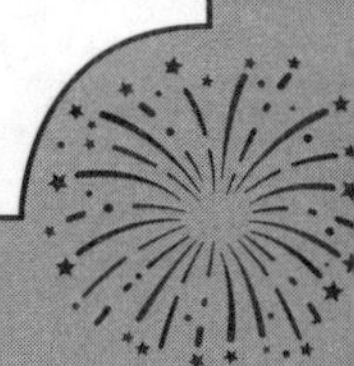

Patriot Prayer

Dear Father,

Even with all that is wrong with America right now, we're still the grandest nation on earth. Thank You for letting me grow up as an American. I love this country with all that is in me, but it makes me so sad to see how it has moved away from You and from the things that made us great. Turn our people back to You. Send a mighty revival throughout our land. Make people wake up and see what's happening, and help them to see that silence is no longer an option if we want future generations to know the America we've known and to have the religious freedom we've experienced.

Amen.

You don't have to watch the news or read posts on social media for long to know that countless groups stay offended by things—and they're quite vocal about it. Fellow patriots, if it doesn't offend and upset you when you see folks making a mockery of and denigrating God, our faith, and our country, then something is wrong. Ask God to show you how you can take a stand for Him. Speak up for what's important. We can't afford to be silent anymore.

CHAPTER FOURTEEN

Humble Hearts

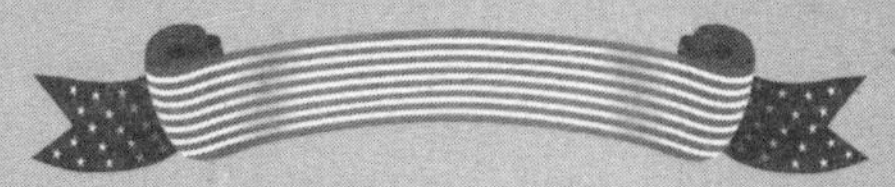

"But he giveth more grace. Wherefore he saith, God resisteth the proud, but giveth grace unto the humble."

—James 4:6 (KJV)

Once upon a time, there lived a king who was very proud. And because this king exalted himself above God, the people of the entire nation suffered. Once upon a time? Isn't that the same old story throughout history, woven in the backdrop of every country?

Yes, we are proud Americans. We love this country. And we should, for not only is it a wonderful country, but many have also given their lives to serve and protect it. We are blessed to call it our home. Pride of country with humility of heart brings people together with strength.

Election years are characterized by a swell of national pride. But the amazing country we live in is such because of a great God. He has opened doors of opportunity and rewarded hard work. He has allowed us to worship freely and pursue God-given interests.

But God requires humility both as a people and as a nation. And it must begin with us individually.

Saul was the first king of Israel. He went from an ordinary man to an arrogant ruler who disobeyed God. King Saul's rapid decline in following God led to an entire nation's decline.

We've all seen it happen with heady political influence, haven't we? Power, fame, and wealth changes how people think. Pride enters and they forget the God who placed them there.

Throughout the Bible, downfall awaited those who succumbed to conceit. We see this demonstrated in the story of King Saul. Samuel, the prophet who had anointed Saul, pronounced a heartbreaking conclusion to Saul's reign—a stark reminder that God desires humble hearts.

In 1 Samuel 13:14b (KJV) God says, "Thou hast not kept *that* which the Lord commanded thee."

In the New Testament, Peter instructs us to be clothed with humility. It should be part of the DNA of the believer. In 1 Peter 5:5–6 (KJV), it tells us, "For God resisteth the proud, and giveth grace to the humble. Humble yourselves therefore under the mighty hand of God, that he may exalt you in due time."

As we consider the wonderful country we live in, we need to pray for humble hearts. There is much arrogance and selfish pride. We hear it shouted from the podiums, and much of it encourages haughtiness, wrong above right, and proclaims evil over good.

We must humble our hearts before God. The spiritual needs of our country cannot be met without submission to Him first in prayer and obedience. God resists the proud. But He gives grace to the humble. May we be people filled with His grace.

1. What characterizes people of humility versus people of pride?
2. Is there a difference between national pride and personal pride? Explain why you think there is or is not.
3. Why does God desire humble hearts?
4. How should 1 Peter 5:5–6 be reflected in your life and political attitudes or actions?

Patriot Prayer

Father,

I know I have often allowed pride to enter my heart and to reign where only You should. You are God alone, and I ask for You to be exalted through my life. Teach me to place You in Your rightful position so that I am then in mine. I pray for our country. May we as a nation humble ourselves under Your mighty hand. Remove conceit and self-exaltation. May our country experience the benefits of a land whose God is the Lord. Show us how to be a people of humble hearts so that others will be drawn to You as the true King of Kings. Thank You for giving us this country as our home.

Amen.

If we want our nation to respond to God's command for humble hearts, we must first be people of humble hearts. Humility is not weakness, but rather a position of yielded strength to what God asks of us. Begin in prayer. Ask God how He wants to work through you. Pray for wisdom. Be informed on the issues. Be prepared to articulate your beliefs. There are so many issues which beg us to stand up for what is right. But friends, to do that in the power of His Spirit and not our own takes time first in His presence. It is in this position of humility that we will prosper and our nation will find hope.

CHAPTER FIFTEEN

Fix Me First

*"Ye have seen what I did unto the Egyptians,
and how I bare you on eagles' wings,
and brought you unto myself."
—Exodus 19:4 (KJV)*

I suppose I'm not alone. As I look at some of the directions in which America seems to be headed, I complain. I find myself whining and upset about decisions made, actions taken, and even about things that should be accomplished but are not.

It feels as though so much in our wonderful United States of America is broken.

Policies which allow and even promote immorality, waste, crime, and hatred grate at my conscience. Double standards seem unjust and intentional. Faith in God is, at times, openly mocked.

As I read the headlines, I hold a running commentary with myself. When I watch the news or scroll the internet, I am dismayed. I know I'm not alone. We share the same troubling concerns, and we hold the same desires for change. And if we had a few moments together, our common denominators would build as we shared our concerns regarding the state of our nation.

But wait, we don't need to stay in despair. Because while many fissures may exist in this great republic of

America, there is so much for which to be grateful. As in many cycles of history throughout the globe, when people have strayed from God, their complaints revealed much about themselves.

Numbers 14:2b (KJV) says, "Would God that we had died in the land of Egypt! or would God we had died in this wilderness!" People complained because they forgot God. They forgot the unprecedented miracles He had done on their behalf. They didn't remember His words to them and how He showed Himself in unmistakable ways.

God yearned for them to realize how much they themselves needed fixing, so that He could bring healing. God wants that for us as well.

When Moses led the children of Israel out of the land of Egypt, they grumbled like petulant children. They begged him to fix their health issues, travel hiccups, dietary and food shortages and dislikes, housing matters, and leadership disputes. Seriously, it seemed as though Moses couldn't get a break.

Their outlook would have been transformed if they had admitted their sin and chosen to obey God. Their nation would have flourished if they had petitioned God to "Fix me first." And our nation would as well.

Yankee Doodle

1. What do you need to fix in your own life so that God's name may be more clearly proclaimed in our great country?
2. What are some things you can thank God for right now concerning our nation even in its brokenness?
3. How might you learn to recognize His goodness even when you disagree with many of the things that are happening in our nation?
4. In what ways can you show obedience to God as a citizen of America?

Patriot Prayer

Father,

Forgive us for despairing about others without fixing ourselves first. Please open our eyes to our own sins and disobediences to which we are blind. Help us to see how much You have blessed us by putting us in this land. Thank You that Your hand of blessing has guided in our past, and we plead with You, that Your hand would guide America again. May our country experience Your spiritual healing and renewal as people put their trust in You. Make us grateful and hopeful because we know You are able to fix our own hearts and the soul of this great nation.

Amen.

There's no better time than today to examine your own heart. What brokenness does God see that you need to deal with, so you will represent Him well to others? Are there bad attitudes or actions you display when you disagree with the way things are run? How can you bring those under God's authority? Are there fears which hinder you from standing firm in obedience to Him when you are confronted with political disputes? This is a good day to seek gratefulness and grace while being bold and effective. It's time to stand against whatever grieves His heart in our nation.

CHAPTER SIXTEEN

The Boy Who Wanted to Make His School Great Again

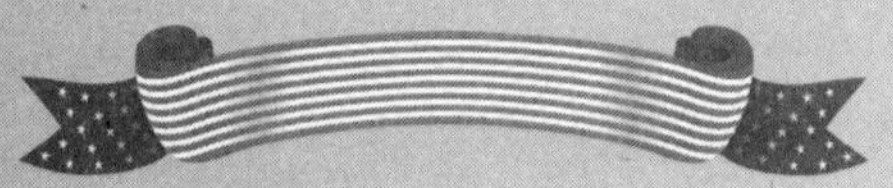

"Even a child is known by his doings,
whether his work be pure,
and whether it be right."
—Proverbs 20:11 (KJV)

Jimmy Heyward was a middle schooler at St. Bonaventure Catholic School in Huntington Beach, California when he made national headlines.

He had aspirations of becoming the school's commissioner of school spirit and patriotism on the student council.

Jimmy put together one mighty fine campaign strategy—one even President Trump would have admired. The young fellow designed a banner and created embroidered red hats all adorned with his campaign message—Make SBS Great Again!

Of course, part of running for office is delivering a stump speech—and Jimmy had written a terrific speech.

He wanted to encourage his classmates to respect America, to know the meaning of the Pledge of Allegiance, and to stop eating nachos during the national anthem.

But Jimmy never got to deliver that speech. That's because school leaders made him remove all the references to patriotism. When Jimmy stood his ground, the school told him he would not be allowed to speak.

The entire episode was meant to shame a little boy whose only crime was to love America. He was silenced because he was a patriot. To make matters worse—the school sent an email to parents and teachers alleging that Jimmy's speech violated the school's Christian Code of Conduct and insinuated he was not respectful or inclusive.

The young boy's plight drew outrage from many—including Elon Musk who wrote a brief message on his X account: "Hating on America is not cool."

Since Jimmy was banned from delivering his remarks at St. Bonaventure, my staff reached out to his mother and she gave me permission to broadcast her son's speech during my Newsmax television program.

"My love for America is my motivation for running for Commissioner of Patriotism and School Spirit," the thirteen-year-old said. "It is an honor to live in this country and sadly some people take their citizenship for granted. Whether it is disrespecting the people who protect us or eating nachos during the national anthem at a sporting event. Many people recite the Pledge of Allegiance without understanding its meaning. If someone doesn't truly know what they are pledging to the United States of America, we might as well be reciting the lyrics to 'Shake It Off' by Taylor Swift. I want to fix this so everyone understands the meaning of the Pledge of Allegiance. As the Commissioner of Patriotism, I would have the crucial task of creating ways to bring more patriotism to SBS. I love my country and I love Saint Bonaventure, but I want to strengthen our patriotism and school spirit. So accordingly, I, Jimmy Heyward, am running for Commissioner of Patriotism and School Spirit. I want to clarify that my ideas are not promises, but I can promise to make pep rallies great again. I will make the school spirit great again. I will make patriotism within SBS be great again. And mostly I will make SBS great again. Thank you and God bless Saint Bonaventure Catholic School."

God bless you, Jimmy! What a terrific speech and what a great reminder of what an amazing nation we have. Ronald Reagan once said that American greatness starts not in Washington, DC, but around the kitchen table.

Jimmy was clearly raised right—taught to love God and country. Traditional values. American values.

Who would ever have thought that a young boy would be reprimanded for being patriotic? For wanting to show respect for our flag and our national anthem? Our ancestors would be stunned.

They'd be even more appalled to discover that God is no longer welcome in most of our schools, and even (by many) in our country.

We proved in this last election that we can be the loud majority. We can't afford to be silent any longer, and when we come together for what's important, we are a powerful force.

Almighty God is the one who has blessed this country so abundantly. We must plant the seeds of faith in this next generation. We must teach them about the God who has made America what it is today, and about those who lived so faithfully before us.

We must teach them about character and respect for God, our country, and others. Yes, that same respect that Jimmy Heyward wanted for his school. I agree with this brave young man. It's time to make our schools great again—and that will begin with making our families great again.

YANKEE DOODLE

1. Why have so many people responded with hatred and disrespect to God and our country—and what can we do about that?
2. How has our silence contributed to that, and why is it so crucial that we return to those values?
3. Why is remembering where we've come from as a country important to our future?
4. Why is it so vital that parents instill faith, values, and character into the lives of their children?

Patriot Prayer

Father,

Many people would give anything to have the rights and freedoms that we have had here in America. The precious right to worship God freely—the very reason the pilgrims came to our great land. For the right to live in freedom in a country they can respect and take pride in. And the right to experience the abundant blessings that God has bestowed on our great nation. But we have taken those things for granted. Our liberty has become tarnished. We've allowed a vocal minority to speak into the minds and hearts of our children, teaching them to disrespect our country and to turn away from God. Wake us up, Lord, and take us back to the values that made this country great.

Amen.

There are plenty of people who would love to teach *their* values to our children—and those are usually values completely opposite our own. Our lives are busy, but we must make the time to pour into our children. They're our greatest investment and the greatest hope for our faith and our country to continue. Teach your children Bible stories, verses, and the old hymns. Teach them strength of character. Teach them by living a godly example in front of them. Plant a love for God and for America in their hearts that they can carry to the next generation. Because we can't afford for someone else to ruin the most awesome gift that God has given to us as parents.

Chocolate Chip Cookie Dough Dip

From the Kitchen of Mrs. Ruby

Ingredients:

- 8 ounces cream cheese, softened
- ½ cup butter, softened (no substitutes)
- ¼ teaspoon vanilla extract
- ¾ cup powdered sugar
- 2 tablespoons brown sugar, packed
- ¾ cup milk chocolate chips (the mini ones work great)
- ¾ cup chopped pecans
- Graham crackers

Directions:

Beat the cream cheese, butter, and vanilla in a mixing bowl until the mixture is fluffy. Add the powdered sugar and the brown sugar. Beat until combined. Stir in the chocolate chips and the chopped pecans. Chill. Serve with graham crackers.

*I always double this recipe. People love this. I sometimes use an assortment of regular graham crackers and chocolate graham crackers for serving.

CHAPTER SEVENTEEN

The Mercy of God

"Be merciful, just as your Father is merciful."
—Luke 6:36 (NASB)

Perhaps, in despair, you've looked at our country and said, "We need a revival."

In many ways, we've become untethered to what has guided our country in the past. We find ourselves in previously unthinkable territory with many politicians supporting principles which oppose biblical faith. We can't let this happen.

Revivals—those sweeping times of turning to God—demonstrate His mercy.

One of the most noted revivals in American history happened between 1730 and 1760, ending about sixteen years before the Declaration of Independence was signed. It undoubtedly influenced the foundations of our great republic.

Great movements of God bring a renewal, restoration, and awareness of spiritual things. We need that, don't we?

Ephesians 2:4–5 (ESV) shares, "But God, being rich in mercy, because of the great love with which he loved us, even when we were dead in our trespasses, made us alive together with Christ—by grace you have been saved." His mercy is rich because His love is great.

Individual revival begins with recognition of sin followed by true humility and repentance. A massive return to God begins the same way. But before revival is birthed in others, it begins with one. Before it can sweep a nation, it must begin with you and me.

Mercy is often described as not receiving the punishment we deserve. For there to be a great turning back to God, there must be a reckoning of our souls' deepest need.

In the Beatitudes, Jesus preached a radical message of mercy. In Luke 6:36 (NASB), He tells us to be merciful. But then He added these words: "...just as your Father is merciful."

The mercy we extend to others comes with this message: our Father is merciful. This is where revival begins. Jesus offers His mercy. It lifts us from death to life in Christ. Spiritual revival cannot happen unless we first embrace God's mercy in our own lives.

Repentance stops pointing at others' sins and shortcomings and acknowledges our own.

Friends, let's pray for revival—one that spreads from a spark of one to a wildfire of many across our nation.

God has shown His mercy in many ways to our great country. We have freedom to worship Him, pray, and speak out about our faith. His mercy can be proclaimed from the pulpit, in print, and in the streets. But bit by bit, these freedoms are being quenched.

God still reaches down to save those who put their trust in Him. May we be among those who proclaim His mercy so that revival sweeps our nation once again.

Yankee Doodle

1. What is your own personal testimony? Can you articulate God's mercy in your own life?
2. What part does repentance play in revival? Why is it so important?
3. What significance does God's mercy have in dealing with those who oppose your beliefs?
4. How would a revival change America?

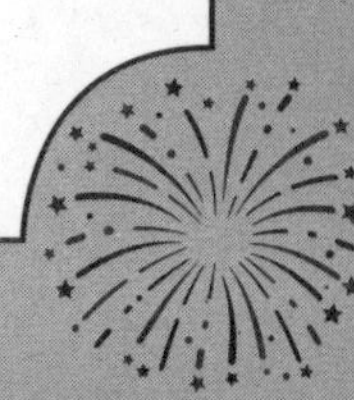

Patriot Prayer

Dear Father,

Send revival. Change my own heart first. Open my eyes to sin in my life. Make me conscious of those times when I do things which displease You. It's easy for me to see the sins of others, but somehow, I'm blind to my own. Father, my own heart needs repentance. I ask for Your mercy and conviction. I ask for forgiveness and change. You are a merciful Father. Thank you for Your love and rich mercy. Please reveal Yourself to the people of this land that there might be a great turning to You. Revive America. Show us Your mercy. Thank You for dying on the cross so mercy can be ours.

Amen.

Become informed about the great American revivals in the past and take note of common denominators. Consider how they influenced the nation. Start prayer groups to pray for revival. Pray for your local leaders, school administrators, and authorities by name. Find a way to let them know you are praying for them. Perhaps send a card or note or find a way to meet them and tell them in person. It is one thing to pray for someone, quite another to follow that up with letting them know it. It may surprise you to find how much it is appreciated.

CHAPTER EIGHTEEN

IF MY PEOPLE

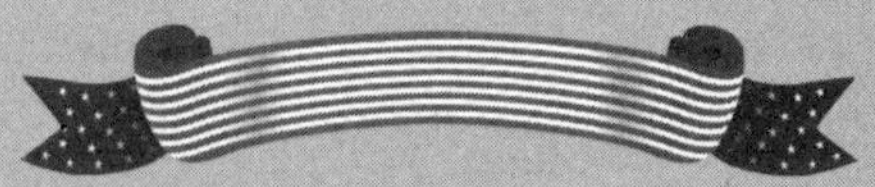

"If my people, who are called by my name,
will humble themselves and pray and seek my
face and turn from their wicked ways,
then I will hear from heaven, and I will forgive
their sin and will heal their land."
—2 Chronicles 7:14 (NIV)

"Mom, I'm such a sinner," a third grader cried as she very dramatically flung herself into her house after a day at school.

As it turned out, she was being quite accurate. She had gone the entire day at school with a paper clip attached to her teeth, appearing remarkably like braces. As she garnered the attention she sought at school that day, and giggled with a hand over her mouth, the lie grew until she began to realize she might need to wear that paper clip for a lifetime.

Or she could admit she lied to her teacher and an entire class. Confession is painful. Humility doesn't come easily. But they are the components of powerful and effective prayer.

At the dedication of Solomon's temple, God gave a beautiful promise for His people. We can learn principles from it for us as well. The verse resurfaces during election cycles and some of our presidents and vice presidents have used this verse while taking the oath of office.

Although the words were addressed to the nation of Israel with whom God had a unique and special covenant, it presents a wonderful pattern as we petition our Heavenly Father for America. Let's humble ourselves in prayer, seek His face, and turn from sin.

James 5:16 (NIV) tells us, "Therefore confess your sins to each other and pray for each other so that you may be healed. The prayer of a righteous person is powerful and effective."

For those who know Christ and belong to Him, we have become part of His family. Not only does He love us dearly as His children, but He grieves over our sin, and wants our relationship with Him to be free from blockages.

There is so much at stake for our country. The crossroads we face will chart a course for our children and grandchildren. They will change our country's trajectory for many years to come. They will decide futures and alter boundaries.

God listens to the humble prayers of His people.

This third-grade girl's repentance was real. The next day her mother accompanied her as she did something difficult but important. She confessed to her teacher and friends what she'd done. It was a hard lesson, but the forgiveness and love she received taught her a precious truth. God forgives the humble. In love, He turns the repentant heart back to Him.

It can begin now for America. As God commanded His covenant nation, we, again, must humble ourselves, pray, seek His face, and turn from sin. And sometimes it takes a little child to lead us.

Yankee Doodle

1. What does it mean to belong to the family of God?
2. How do you react when you become aware of sin which hinders your relationship with the Father?
3. James 5:16 talks about confessing sin to one another and praying for one another. In what ways do you follow James's teaching for corporate prayer?
4. How could you incorporate the pattern of prayer given in 2 Chronicles 7:14?

Patriot Prayer

Dear Father,

It's so difficult to admit when we sin, but Lord, as a nation and as Your people, we certainly have. We seek Your face. We ask for the power to turn from our wicked ways. We recognize that spiritual healing is our deepest need. We pray that You would help us to be obedient children, to follow Your commands, and to grow to be more like You. Help us to encourage one another, and to be in unity as the body of Christ as we confess our sins, and as we pray for one another and for America. Help us lift one another up. Show us how to be a testimony in our nation that will draw people to You. Thank you, Father, for Your forgiveness.

Amen.

Our verse in James affirms the practice of corporate prayer. If you meet with someone for regular prayer times, don't forget to pray for our nation. Begin a group specifically for prayer using the pattern given in 2 Chronicles 7:14. Commit to starting with a time of shared confession. As God says in Proverbs 27:17 (NKJV), "Iron sharpens iron." Let's find others concerned about our nation and dedicate ourselves together in earnest prayer for our country.

CHAPTER NINETEEN

A Strong Defense

"The name of the Lord is a strong tower;
the righteous run to it and are safe."
—Proverbs 18:10 (NKJV)

There was a town in northern Italy that had ancient defense systems. They were towers. Tall, narrow, and straight, they were made of hewn rock laboriously laid one upon another. Impenetrable. Unknock-down-able.

In the twelfth and thirteenth centuries, when enemy armies came to invade, the people would run to their nearest tower to be safe. It was their strong defense against harm.

Our nation prides itself on its strong defense. Our branches of military are well-trained and prepared. We have the highest levels of technology. We are considered a formidable enemy for those who would seek to harm us.

But often the strongest defenses are not ones we can see with our eyes. They are the invisible things of God.

In our nation, our strong spiritual defenses are being challenged daily. In many ways, God is no longer at the top. Other gods have replaced Him. Weaker gods. And it renders us weaker as a nation, without defense. We fear the impact on those coming behind us.

Sometimes, we can't help but wonder where our strong towers went.

It's easy to sling blame, but are we also letting down our eternal defenses? Are we building the kind of strength which endures? Are we intentionally passing down a legacy of faith through prayer, meeting together as a body of Christ, and Bible reading?

In our political climate, we may feel that we have our defenses ready. Perhaps we've diligently studied the issues which plague our country. We are aware of the foundations which are under attack and know how best to defend our viewpoints.

The Apostle Paul was a master of defending the faith while he lived in a political mess. He spoke to religious leaders, governors, magistrates, council members, and ranking officers.

But one of the most sinister rulers ever had Christians on his radar. Nero, the powerful Roman emperor, persecuted Christians, while he himself sank into an ever-deepening insanity.

Paul wrote how to live in relationship to the political climate in which he lived. "I urge, then, first of all, that petitions, prayers, intercession and thanksgiving be made for all people—for kings and all those in authority, that we may live peaceful and quiet lives in all godliness and holiness." 1 Timothy 2:1–2 (NIV)

Earthly defenses cannot withstand forever. Most of those indestructible towers in Italy have been removed or shortened. Where once the horizon was filled with them, few remain.

Let's make sure our strong defense is the name of the Lord. Let's petition Him for our country's spiritual strength. No other tower will ever be so strong.

Yankee Doodle

1. In what ways do you experience God as your strong tower in this political climate?
2. How have you found prayer to be a strong defense?
3. What was Paul's purpose in praying for kings and those in authority? Why do you think he asked for those specific things?
4. How can you incorporate the next generation into your prayer habits?

Patriot Prayer

Dear Father,

Thank You for being our strong tower. We need You to defend us. We need You to return as the strength of our nation. We confess that as a country, we have strayed and sinned against You. We have trusted in other things, policies, leaders, and laws. We have put them as our place to run to for safety. We want the name of the Lord to be our strong tower. When we see things in our nation that cause us to worry and fear, help us cling to You. We pray for those who rule over us, that their leadership would allow Your people to live peaceful and quiet lives in all godliness and holiness.

Amen.

Pray regularly with others of like-minded faith "for kings and all those in authority, that we may live peaceful and quiet lives in all godliness and holiness." List their names. Paul discovered firsthand that when government destroys our mandate to live our lives in a Christ-like manner, chaos erupts. Yet, as Paul learned in those dank, dark prison cells he spent so much time in, the name of the Lord truly did remain his strong high tower. May we follow Paul's prayers with the same confidence. And may we call on the name of the Lord together. He is our strong tower.

CHAPTER TWENTY

The Fraternity Brothers of the University of North Carolina

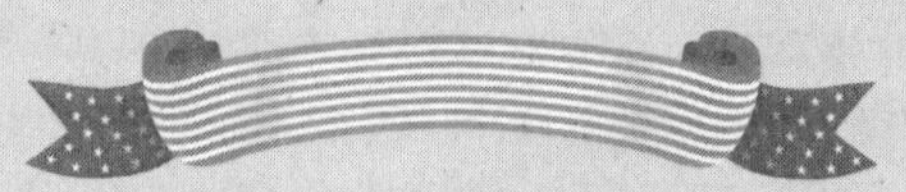

"Be watchful, stand firm in the faith,
act like men, be strong."
—1 Corinthians 16:13 (ESV)

During the Spring of 2024, many American university campuses were rocked by violence committed by pro-Palestinian mobs. Jewish students were chased and beaten. Campus buildings were occupied and a number of American flags were desecrated.

It was no different on the beautiful campus of the University of North Carolina in Chapel Hill. One day, the pro-Hamas mob had stormed the quad and ripped down Old Glory. The flag was replaced with a Palestinian flag. University officials were able to restore the Stars and Stripes, but soon, the mob surged again.

This time, a group of fraternity brothers—many representing a Jewish fraternity—decided that enough was enough. The young men intervened and prevented the mob from desecrating the flag.

Imagine their surprise when they discovered that Chancellor Lee Roberts was in their bunch—defying the mob.

"This university doesn't belong to a small group of protesters," Chancellor Roberts said as protesters screamed obscenities. "It belongs to every citizen of North

Carolina—everybody in North Carolina. The flag represents all of us."

Instead of dispersing, the mob hurled rocks and bottles at the fraternity brothers. But the young men stood their ground.

"The scene that stood before us was just awful," fraternity brother Jacob Harris told Chabad.org. "The same people that had promoted their protest as peaceful were pelting us with all sorts of projectiles—a metal water bottle gave my friend a black eye simply for standing up for his identity and defending the Stars and Stripes. The American flag is a symbol of freedom—the freedom represented by that flag allows me to express my identity just as it allows individuals to protest. Seeing the flag being taken down by the same people that it gives the right to protest felt like a slap in the face of every American citizen," Jacob recounted.

Other students were emboldened by the actions of the "Frat Bros" and soon they chanted, "USA, USA."

"To take down that flag and put up another flag, no matter what other flag it is, that's antithetical to who we are, what this University stands for [and] what we have done for 229 years," the chancellor boldly declared.

Word of the courageous actions of the frat boys spread to other university campuses and it became a rallying cry at the Republican National Convention in Milwaukee, Wisconsin.

"Too many people have sacrificed everything for it," fraternity brother Alex Johnson said in a speech to Republican delegates. "The least we could do was keep it flying, and tonight we are proud to honor our flag again."

Throughout the course of history, men and women have been faced with a choice: do you stand up to evil? Dietrich Bonhoeffer, the German theologian, once admonished Christians, saying, "Silence in the face of evil is evil itself.... Not to speak is to speak. Not to act is to act."

The scene at UNC Chapel Hill was reminiscent of a speech delivered by President Ronald Reagan. He pointed out that our national anthem starts with a question instead of a declaration. Is the flag still there? Can you still see the flag flying?

It's a question every generation of Americans must answer. Are we willing to stand up and fight for freedom and the values that flag represents?

The fraternity brothers at the University of North Carolina responded not with powdered wigs and muskets, but chinos and iPhones. Yes, thanks to their bravery, the Star-Spangled Banner still waves over the land of the free and the home of the brave.

1. Many times throughout the Bible, individuals encountered opportunities where they had to take a stand for what was right. The fraternity brothers did the same. How do you think you would respond if faced with a similar scenario?

2. As the fraternity brothers observed what happened on their campus, they knew they *must* take a stand for what was right. It helped having others with them. How can having brothers and sisters in Christ help to give us confidence and strength when we're required to take a stand?

3. Dietrich Bonhoeffer said, "Silence in the face of evil is evil itself." Can you think of a time when you should have taken a stand—but you didn't?

4. How can you prepare yourself to take a stand for your faith and your country?

Patriot Prayer

Father,

After the horrific stories and images from the Holocaust, I never imagined that Your chosen people would ever be chased and attacked in the streets of America. My heart is grieved for them and for the hatred which has become so prevalent in our country and in our world. Fill me with the resolve and strength I need so that I can and will take a stand for what's right. Silence is not a choice. Help me to act when needed. Give me the courage of my convictions. Lord, bless this great nation. Help my children and grandchildren to know a land where our faith and freedoms are protected by brave Americans.

Amen.

For too long, we've been content to stand on the sidelines and be silent as our freedoms have been trampled, and as respect and pride in America have been stomped out. But when we see our fellow citizens suffering, when we see them arrested and jailed for taking a stand for their religious beliefs, we must be brave and speak out. Find three Christian friends who will pray regularly with you for our country and our religious freedoms. As "iron sharpens iron," may you become friends with those who will be ready and prepared to take a stand together should the need arise.

Billie's "Gotta Have One More" Cookies

From the Kitchen of Billie Fulton

Ingredients:

1 cup butter, softened
1 ¼ cup packed brown sugar
½ cup sugar
2 eggs, room temperature
2 tablespoons milk
2 teaspoons vanilla
1 ¾ cups all-purpose flour
1 teaspoon baking soda
½ teaspoon salt
2 ¾ cups oats
2 cups Ghirardelli milk chocolate chips
1 cup toasted pecans, chopped coarsely after toasting

Directions:

Preheat the oven to 350 degrees. Mix together the butter, brown sugar, and sugar until creamy. Add the eggs, milk, and vanilla; beat well. Stir the flour, baking soda, and salt together and then add to the mixing bowl. Mix well. Then with a large spoon add the oats, chocolate chips, and toasted pecans. Blend well, and then scoop the dough with an ice cream scoop and place on a lightly-greased cookie sheet. Leave the dough rounded (don't pat it down). Bake at 350 degrees for 10–12 minutes or until the cookies are golden brown.

Note: These cookies are dangerous, folks! They're huge, delicious, and impossible to resist.

CHAPTER TWENTY-ONE

In God We Trust

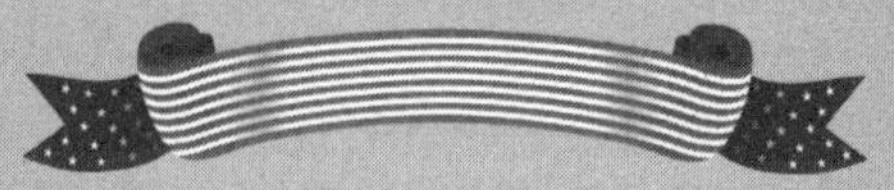

"Trust in the Lord with all your heart."
—Proverbs 3:5a (NIV)

It was a closed fist, but it held magic inside. I remember my daddy slowly opening his hand. There on his palm lay a shiny coin. He flipped it over and pointed to something on the face of it, so tiny I squinted to see what it was.

"What does it say?" he asked.

In my newly acquired reader's tongue, I labored over the minute inscription one word at a time.

"In...God...We...Trust," I finally worked out. "Why, Daddy? Why does it say that?"

I don't recall his answer, but I remember the awe that struck my heart at the greatness of our country. This big land with its important leaders honored God by putting His name on that coin.

Perhaps a parent or teacher once revealed the same inscription to you? You may have shown it to your own children or grandchildren.

There is a tiny bit of history inscribed with words on each American coin. But even more important, it represents an American heritage which recognized true value.

From the Civil War forward, various coins adopted the motto "In God We Trust." But it wasn't until President Eisenhower signed it into law in 1955, that it became a requirement for all bills and coins to bear the inscription.

Oh, that we would once again—like our forefathers—consider our nation's political and economic blessings which are connected to spiritual faith.

That tiny coin still packs a powerful message.

Maybe today there might be few who are aware that "In God We Trust" is our national motto. And perhaps we might question if America still holds to its message.

The Psalms often remind us to place our trust in the Lord. King David proclaimed God his strength, shield, and trust. Isaiah reminds us to trust in God and not be afraid. Jesus tells us in John 14:1 to trust in God, and to trust also in Him.

Trusting God is fundamental to the Christian faith. To know Him, we must put our trust in Him. This is where our true value as a nation lies. Not in government made with our own hands, or in laws or rules formed by human reasoning, but in God.

It's been a while since a shiny coin has slowly unfurled its magic from my hand. It's time.

"Hey boys!" I call my grandsons to my side.

I hold out my closed fist and slowly open it. There, a shiny new coin lies in my palm.

"What does it say, boys?" I ask. They squint as I point to the tiny words. They sound it out, each word at a time. And I see the triumph in their eyes, and the smiles on their faces.

"In God We Trust!"

Yankee Doodle

1. In what ways does America show its belief or unbelief in God?
2. What does trust in God mean to you?
3. How does our national motto connect to our values today?
4. Can you think of specific ways to open a conversation with others about trusting in God?

Patriot Prayer

Dear Father,

Thank You for reminding us about what is of true value. We are grateful for the heritage of placing trust in God as a nation, but we recognize how far we have come from that today. Please help us to get back on track, each one of us individually, and together as a country. Remind us to share with our children, grandchildren, friends, and neighbors, that You are trustworthy. You are the only worthy One. You will never abuse our trust. Thank You for those leaders before us who pointed the way with a spiritual foundation inscribed on our bills and coins. Thank You that "In God We Trust" offers us a testimony of hope.

Amen.

Do you know a child who might benefit from the magic of a coin inscribed with the words "In God We Trust"? Plan a moment for them to find those tiny words and read them. Then, tell them about people who lived a long time ago with such a deep faith that they wanted us to know that God is a God of trust, even many years later. If you have the opportunity to share with an older person, perhaps they would like the reminder as well. Think of other ways to take advantage of the tiny gospel tracts printed on our American currency.

CHAPTER TWENTY-TWO

SEEK GOD'S FACE

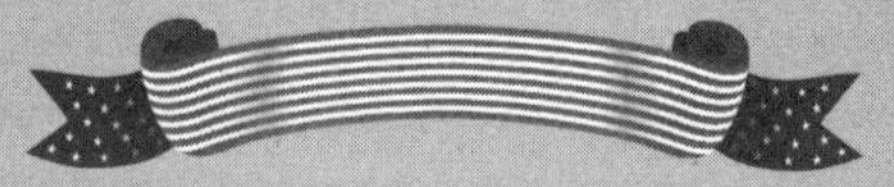

"Seek the Lord and His strength;
Seek His face continually."
—Psalm 105:4 (NASB)

A few Sundays ago, I sat behind our pastor's wife. From my seat, I could see her reactions and read her expressions. As her husband preached, it was obvious that she was his biggest fan. She enjoyed his stories, and her face was so sweet as he explained the Scriptures. It was almost as precious to watch her as it was to listen to our pastor behind the pulpit. Love was on display.

Our faces show so much about what is happening in our hearts. They reveal a lot about our character. Our faces often expose our joys and sorrows, what we hope others see, and what we wish we could hide.

My grandchildren's faces display delight at a new toy, dismay at bedtime, and admiration at their big brother's accomplishments. Their unique personalities and character traits are evident through their expressions. And sometimes, as a grandma, I need to put my face very close to theirs to look into their eyes, so they know how deeply they are loved.

When we love someone, we seek to be in their presence, we desire to know their character, and we revel in bringing them pleasure.

Oh my, how far our nation has traveled from that heartfelt display of love for God. How different would things be if we truly sought God's face in united humbleness? We have shut Him out of our activities, programs, and our children's schools. We have removed His name and erased His history. How can the generations possibly benefit from what they don't know? How can we impart a heart that seeks God's face?

In the Old Testament, the word "face" implies a turning toward Him, to look and be in His presence. He wants us to find Him, to be near and bask in His presence.

God instructs us to seek His face because He desires a deep intimate relationship with us, which comes from spending time with Him.

Our faces reflect His to the world. But when we neglect to meet with Him, that reflection dims.

God's Word reveals His character. As we read the Bible, we learn of His love, mercy, compassion, and kindness. He invites us to be students of His, to learn of Him, and be instructed as disciples. The more we bask in His presence, the more we want to seek Him. And the more we learn of Him, the clearer our reflection of Him will be.

Let's return. Let's seek His face and sit in His presence. Let's open God's Word again and read it. Let's look to Him that He might shine on this great nation again. We certainly need the light of Jesus on our country.

Yankee Doodle

1. How does your life display a person who seeks God? What would enhance that?
2. Our verse says to "seek His face continually." What does that mean and how can you do that?
3. What do you think would be different if our nation would seek God's face, and what benefits would there be for our country?
4. How can you encourage others to seek God's face?

Patriot Prayer

Dear Father,

Thank You for wanting to spend time with us. Forgive us for not seeking Your face, for skimping on that intimacy You long for. Impress Your character on our hearts. Help us to learn to know You better through the pages of Your Word, and to worship You because You are all You claim to be. Help me to resist seeking other things, and draw me to seek You more than anything or any other affection. I pray for this country, I pray that once again we would seek Your face, and honor You with our hearts. Teach us to love You wholly and to bask in Your presence continually. Bind our hearts with Yours and may our adoration be to You alone.

Amen.

When is the last time you sat at Jesus's feet to read His Word and talk to Him? I hope your answer reveals that it is a continual habit, but if not, you are in for a marvelous treat, because God desires to meet with you. Find a quiet space and spend some time looking into the Bible for the character and attributes of God. Write them down in alphabetical order. A: Awesome, B: Blessed, C: Cornerstone. Keep the list handy and available. Add to it as you discover others. Pray each one out loud in worship. You will discover that as God's character becomes more present in your mind, you will seek to be with Him more, and to be more like Him. And if all of us will do that, it will surely impact our country.

CHAPTER TWENTY-THREE

United We Stand

"...that there be no divisions among you,
but that you be perfectly joined together in the
same mind and in the same judgment."
—1 Corinthians 1:10b (NKJV)

Politicians love to talk about a platform which unites. "United we stand, divided we fall," we hear them say to the cheers of their audiences.

The phrase is illustrated by our favorite football teams, inspired by our work teams, and proven by little boys building with blocks on my living room floor.

"No, don't put the red one there, it will make the others fall." A conglomeration of colored blocks—red, yellow, blue, and green—scattered the floor. What started with a tower has now turned into a house, with its top-heavy demise imminent.

"It's gonna be as tall as you," the littlest said to his big brother.

The second-born decided it needed rooms, doors, and a roof.

Divided vision set them up for a colossal fall.

"No, you can't do that," moans the oldest.

What took them so long to build was demolished in seconds.

Unity sounds good from the stage. What unites is key. Promised unity becomes fragmented by differences of understanding.

The history of our nation had division flowing in its veins. People split over issues. Wars were fought and blood was shed. Our Founding Fathers often were polarized in opposing political debate. They faced hostility and opposition—even with each other.

The phrase "United we stand, divided we fall" is attributed to John Dickinson who wrote a pre-revolutionary song containing that thought. Founding Father Patrick Henry famously used the phrase in his final speech. During Lincoln's senate race, he spoke of America as a "house divided." His speech began with, "A house divided against itself cannot stand."

Unifying with what seeks to demolish the biblical foundations of our country will ultimately defeat us. Unrighteousness suppresses truth. As followers of Christ, we should seek a political unity which doesn't oppose God's teachings.

The church in Corinth had divisions. When its moral structure weakened, the pagan culture infiltrated. It brought disunity because they were detached from God's truth. In 1 Corinthians 1:10, Paul speaks of unity through biblical morality rather than philosophical beliefs.

The church is divided today by political thoughts and ideals. Church unity comes through understanding God's Word and being instructed by it. For the body of Christ to be joined together with the same mind, we must pursue biblical truth and values. With strong biblical footing, the philosophical nonsenses of the world will not sway us.

"You can rebuild it," I assured my grandsons while they played the construction-fail blame-game. "The trick is to always get the foundation right."

Yankee Doodle

1. Where do you find the most unity?
2. In what way do the foundational biblical doctrines your church teaches help you with personal political choices?
3. What was Paul referring to in 1 Corinthians 1:10, and how do you see it as applicable to your church and your life?
4. What do you think would help unify our country?

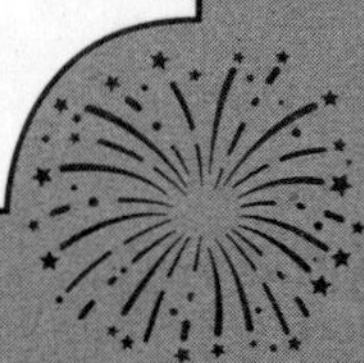

Patriot Prayer

Dear Father,

The cries for unity from our politicians seem like a hopeless call. The polarization of ideas and policies move us farther and farther apart. Lord, we don't want to be in synch with much of it because it dishonors You. Please help us to understand Your Word accurately. Make our roots deep in what You say so that we do not become misled by what mere humans promise. I know You always keep Your promises. Thank You, Lord, that You can be trusted in all You say and in all You do. Teach me Your Word. I pray for church and national unity and against division. Help us to be perfectly joined together in the same mind and in the same judgment. Give us Your desires that Your will might be done.

Amen.

Look at which political promises you feel will be divisive to church unity. It may help to list the issues where you feel unity would not agree with Scripture. Be ready to draw the lines which biblical instruction defines. Find passages of Scripture which help you to encourage unity in others. Ask God to help you see things through His eyes and to guard your heart from a stubborn or prideful attitude. Learn to listen rather than argue. Be interested in why someone holds an opposite position and, if that person is a believer, find out how Scripture has influenced his or her beliefs. Make sure your own foundation is secure in what God's Word says.

CHAPTER TWENTY-FOUR

The Day President Eisenhower Was Baptized

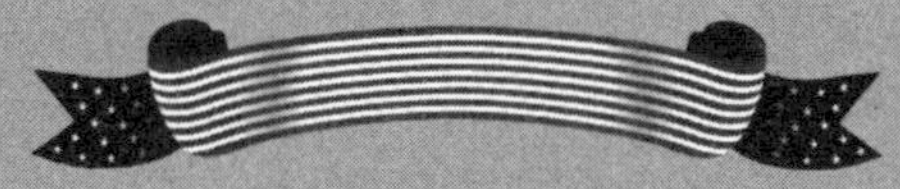

"You yourselves are our letter, written on our hearts, known and read by everyone. You show that you are a letter from Christ, the result of our ministry, written not with ink but with the Spirit of the living God, not on tablets of stone but on tablets of human hearts."
—2 Corinthians 3:2–3 (NIV)

President Dwight Eisenhower was one of the most devout Christians to occupy the Oval Office. He was truly an American hero best known for his role as the Supreme Commander of the Allied Forces during World War II.

But his influence in encouraging Americans to seek a relationship with God is one of history's most untold stories.

Eisenhower is the only president to be baptized after he took the Oath of Office. Just ten days after he put his hand on the Bible, Ike was baptized by the Reverend Edward Elson at National Presbyterian Church.

He was also the first president to open his inaugural address with a prayer. It was an unprecedented act of public religiosity.

"Almighty God, as we stand here at this moment my future associates in the executive branch of government join me in beseeching that Thou will make full and complete our dedication to the service of the people in this throng, and their fellow citizens everywhere. Give us, we pray, the power to discern clearly right from wrong, and allow all our words and actions to be governed thereby, and by the laws of this land. Especially we pray that our concern shall be for all the people regardless of station, race, or calling. May cooperation be permitted and be the mutual aim of those who, under the concepts of our Constitution, hold to differing political faiths; so that all may work for the good of our beloved country and Thy glory. Amen."

Eisenhower's faith journey began as a small child in the fertile faith fields of Abilene, Kansas. His parents were Mennonites who later became Jehovah's Witnesses. But it was the teaching and preaching of Billy Graham that ultimately stirred Ike's personal walk with God.

Jack Holl, the author of *The Religious Journey of Dwight D. Eisenhower*, noted that "for Eisenhower, the very existence of the United States confirmed God's benevolent presence." Eisenhower believed that "democracy made no logical sense without the recognition of a Supreme Being, as the Founding Fathers acknowledged."

During his eight years in office, Ike signed a bill adding the phrase "under God" to the Pledge of Allegiance. He also signed a bill declaring "In God We Trust" as the nation's motto. The law also mandated the phrase be printed on all of our currency.

Eisenhower was instrumental in establishing the National Prayer Breakfast. He backed the American Legion's

"Back to God" campaign and he started every Cabinet meeting with a moment of silence.

Paul Batura, a writer for Focus on the Family, noted that by the end of Eisenhower's administration, church attendance had increased from 49 percent to 69 percent.

President Eisenhower understood that a relationship with God was the key to making our nation great. And he set a tremendous example during his time in office.

In 1954, he emphasized the importance of godliness and spirituality in American history from George Washington in prayer at Valley Forge to Abraham Lincoln fighting to save the Union. The History Channel theorized that Eisenhower believed religious faith was the "single most important distinction between American freedom and Communist oppression."

To this day, not much is known about the baptism ceremony at National Presbyterian Church. His wife, Mamie, was a longtime member of the Presbyterian denomination. But since the ceremony itself was private, the American people will forever be left to wonder if our thirty-fourth president was sprinkled or dunked.

1. Dwight D. Eisenhower was a president who truly wanted to acknowledge God in our country. His faith was impacted by the preaching and teaching of Dr. Billy Graham. What can you learn about the power of example from these two men?
2. What are five important things you can take away from President Eisenhower's incredible prayer that opened his inaugural address, and what difference do you think it would make if our elected officials all ruled under those principles?
3. What happened with church attendance because of his influence in encouraging Americans to seek a relationship with God?
4. President Eisenhower understood that a relationship with God was the key to making our nation great. Is your personal relationship with God helping to make your community and your nation great? And if not, what do you need to do to make that happen?

PATRIOT PRAYER

Father,

The example of President Eisenhower inspires me. Give us leaders who will do likewise. Help me to pray faithfully for the elected officials of our country. Give them bold courage to take a stand for You, to lead our nation so that our citizens will follow in Your footsteps. To a place where God will be honored in our land again. Turn hearts back to You. Fill the pews in our churches again. Give us families of faith again. I'm certainly not in a position of power such as President Eisenhower was, but I can still be a leader and inspire others to return to You and to serve You. Help me to be faithful to do that. Make America godly again, Lord. Do it again.

Amen.

President Eisenhower's prayer touched my heart immensely. Over the next seven days, find time to pray that prayer each day. Highlight a different clause from that prayer each day and ask God to speak to your heart through those words. Do it as a family as well. Discuss the thoughts that President Eisenhower expressed so well in this prayer, and then talk about how that affects you as a family. All of us have a responsibility to serve God and our country. Can you imagine the difference that would make in our beloved country if all of us would become sensitive to God's leading as was portrayed in the life of this godly leader?

Strawberry Tea

From the Kitchen of Aunt Rainey (Lorraine Sherlin)

Ingredients:

1 ½ quarts of water
Three family-size tea bags (or nine regular-size tea bags)
10 ounces frozen strawberries
1 small can frozen lemonade
½ cup sugar (adjust to your taste)
2-liter lemon-lime soft drink

Directions:

Bring the water to a boil. Add the tea bags. Turn the burner off immediately, but leave the pan on the burner for ten minutes for the tea to steep.

Puree the frozen strawberries. Then, add the strawberries, frozen lemonade, and the half cup of sugar to the tea. Chill. At serving time, add the two liters of the lemon-lime soft drink. Stir well; enjoy.

CHAPTER TWENTY-FIVE

For Such a Time as This

"Be very careful, then, how you live—not as unwise but as wise, making the most of every opportunity, because the days are evil."
—Ephesians 5:15–16 (NIV)

Sometimes I feel as if I'm walking on eggshells. I wonder if you've felt that too. My patriotism and loyalty for our country seems at political odds with the views of many others. I worry my children and grandchildren will absorb a culture bent on destroying the principles we hold dear.

But as I sometimes wring my hands and wonder what can be done, as I mourn and grieve for the things which hurt our Father, I can miss an important truth. In every country, God has placed His people for a divine purpose.

Are we then living wise and careful lives so that God can use us even as we observe our nation's spiritual decline? A peek in the Bible at the life of Esther shows us a powerful example of how to live as believers in our country today. Displaced from her own people and home, she must have felt out of place at times—both spiritually and culturally. But Esther, by God's design, became the queen of Persia.

A political conspiracy plotted to annihilate the Jewish people to whom she belonged. Mordecai, Esther's relative and childhood guardian, challenged her to overcome her fear and go to the king to stop the conspiracy. In Esther 4:14b (ESV), he asks her, "And who knows whether you have not come to the kingdom for such a time as this?"

Friends, we are at a crux in our history, too. As we stand in this gap, we must also see that it is no accident we are in America at this specific time.

We must not let fear stand in our way. Our lives have great purpose when we live them boldly for Him. Yet, we must be careful to obey Him and to take every opportunity to proclaim His name.

Esther accepted the call. She was willing to lay down her life in the hope of saving her people. "If I perish, I perish," she declared in Esther 4:16b (ESV)

God helped Esther. He gave her wisdom and the right words to say. We often struggle with what to say or how to speak up about what we believe. We might feel afraid, but God can and will help us.

Will you also accept the call to a strong faith regardless of our political sinking sands? If we expect to make a difference in this great country, we must live ready to serve, even at our own risk. As Ephesians 5:16b (NIV) instructs, let's make "the most of every opportunity, because the days are evil."

Fellow patriots, we were born for such a time as this. Lord, help us to be as faithful as Esther.

Yankee Doodle

1. What fears do you face in confronting political situations? How can those fears impact those situations?
2. What do you think today's verse is talking about when it tells us to be careful?
3. How does the political situation of Esther's day correspond to ours now?
4. How has God helped you when encountering disagreements over political issues with others?

Patriot Prayer

Father,

Sometimes it's hard to know what to say, or if I should say anything at all. Help me speak when You want me to and be silent when it is wise. Teach me to live a careful life in this evil world. Give us wisdom. Set us apart as Your followers so that we can represent You well. Give us occasions to share the gospel of Jesus and give us the right words at the right time. Keep us from allowing fear to rob us of taking those opportunities when You want us to share. Holy Spirit, convict others and help them to turn to You. Help us to fulfill Your purpose in our lives for such a time as this. Help us to follow Esther's example of faithfulness.

Amen.

Taking action means not allowing lethargy or apathy to rule. It negates the feeling of, "What's the use?" or "What difference can I make?" Think of neighbors or friends with whom you have not yet shared Christ and write down their names. Pray over each of them that their hearts would be receptive to truth. Ask God for opportunities to spread His good news. Live for Jesus in such a way that He shines brighter and clearer than political viewpoints. All of us need to remember that we are called for such a time as this.

CHAPTER TWENTY-SIX

OLD GLORY

"The apostles left…rejoicing because they had been counted worthy of suffering disgrace for the Name."
—Acts 5:41 (NIV)

A small group of friends from our church met for a Bible study. We walked into a discussion which led to politics. "Things have never been so bad in our country," one of the older ladies bemoaned.

"What are you talking about?" a student from a prestigious university responded with shock. "I've never seen so many students open to talk about Jesus on campus."

The seasoned woman compared her country with a time when it was customary for political debate to be tethered to belief in God. She missed the former glory days and longed for a return to them.

The twenty-something medical student responded to the current situation as "just regular life." For her, America's old glory didn't connect with today. It was just...old.

However, as unrest, confusion, turmoil, and craziness flew off the rails on her campus, the student saw the political climate as contributing to a rising spiritual hunger. Students longed for something politics could not offer.

When we think of Old Glory, our mind's eye goes to the flag. It's a revered symbol of God and country, patriotism and pride. Red, white, and blue, it stands tall and waves majestically. It brings our hands to our hearts and gives voice to our allegiance. We offer it a moment of honor and respect at sports events, schools, concerts, and churches. We love the flag of the United States of America.

We want our young people to feel the same patriotic swell in their hearts, but many see something else. We want them to know a country whose respect for the flag is connected to reverence for God, but few make that connection.

We cannot simply stand still on the shoulders of Old Glory while we mourn for the past.

In my young friend's world, the revered history of our country has been changed. It occupies a very dim and murky space. And it makes us sad.

But I also see joy. Because while we glimpse proof of the degradation and hopelessness of our political reality, she sees this mess as an opportunity for the gospel. She is ready like the apostles to be counted worthy of Christ even on American soil.

It is imperative that we share true history with our younger generation. It's important we tell stories of our patriots and pass down our love for this country. But we also must be willing to move from complaining to actively coming alongside our Christian young people in the fray. Seasoned patriots, we must help them approach their world through the grid of God's Word, so that their lives may be lived for God's glory.

1. In what ways do you see young people politically involved?
2. In our verse today, the apostles rejoiced in their suffering. How would you feel and react under the same circumstances?
3. What makes you sad about how some young people view patriotism?
4. What does it mean to interpret politics through the grid of God's Word?

Patriot Prayer

Dear Father,

We need You so much in this world we live in. We are concerned about our country and worried about its influence on the next generation. We see the degradation and moral decline, and we don't want our children and grandchildren to fall into its evil. Protect them. Protect us. Help us to meet together in Your Word. Give us wisdom in approaching their world view with them, to be gentle and kind, yet uncompromising in right and wrong. Help us to strengthen them not only to stand strong through the destructive thinking that's so prevalent in our country, but to rejoice in the opportunity to suffer for Christ if need be. May our children and grandchildren be counted worthy and willing to give their lives for Your glory.

Amen.

Do you know how to share the gospel with someone else? Have you equipped anyone else to do that? Now is a great time to take a class, do a study, online course, or start an evangelism class in your church. Whichever way politics leads us in the future, we cannot deny that it has always had a part in the freedom or restriction of spreading the gospel. We need to be aware of how to approach politics through the truth of Scripture. And we must befriend young people, bridge the gap with coffee or a meal, and listen to them. They will be the next generation to lead our country.

CHAPTER TWENTY-SEVEN

There Are No Atheists in Foxholes

"For I am not ashamed of the gospel of Christ, for it is the power of God to salvation for everyone who believes, for the Jew first and also for the Greek."
—Romans 1:16 (NKJV)

A soldier remembers the distinguished, graying Navy chaplain introducing himself during one of the first Sunday services. It was the beginning of the war, Operation Desert Storm, and apprehensive military personnel of all ages and ranks gathered under the tent. Chaplain Smith stood behind a makeshift pulpit and recounted the events that led to his current position as a chaplain.

Turns out, this wasn't his first war. Chaplain Smith served as a Marine during the Vietnam War. In a tragic and terrifying battle, every person in Smith's unit was killed except for him. Close friends, comrades, and fellow Marines—his entire unit wiped out.

"In some of the final moments of my friends' lives here on earth, I heard them call out to God. Some, I'm not sure they'd ever said that word without an expletive following it. Many were devout believers the entire time I knew them. A couple of them begged God to save them.

"I'm not sure who first said, 'There are no atheists in foxholes,'" Smith continued. "I think I once heard it was attributed to a war correspondent. But I can almost promise you that before this war is over, you will be calling out to the God who created you, the one who created this entire universe. The one true God of the Bible.

Because whether you've loved Him for as long as you can remember or denied Him for most of your life—He is real. He is God. And while you're here under these conditions, you probably need Him more than you've ever needed God before in your life."

Following the Vietnam War, Smith left the Marine Corps to attend military chaplain school. Though he struggled to recover from losing his entire unit, Smith returned to the service as a Navy chaplain to do all he could to help military personnel find and hang onto God—especially during their darkest time of need.

Fellow comrades, we need God in this nation more than we've ever needed Him before. Many Christians have drifted away from Him and have become lukewarm believers. Too many former believers have turned their backs on God completely, denying He ever existed. Some have never even heard the name Jesus Christ. And many don't have a clue nor do they care what they believe about God.

Friends, our nation is in a foxhole right now. We've practically turned our soil into the trenches of "us" versus "them" with a lot of "thems" out there. We need God now. Don't wait until it's too late to call on him. Call on God now and believe. Ask Him to restore your faith and turn your heart back to Him. Don't be ashamed of Christ, because He is the only answer for salvation—and the only answer for our country.

Yankee Doodle

1. How does what our nation has been going through make you feel as if you've been in a foxhole?
2. What can you say about Jesus to those who are in the trenches with you daily?
3. Have the battles you've faced in our country recently weakened or strengthened your faith?
4. Do you know someone who needs to hear about Jesus Christ for the first time?

Patriot Prayer

Dear God,

Sometimes it feels like we are in a battle right here on our own soil. A battle to save our children and the next generation from falling away from You completely. Heavenly Father, please help me fight to save my children and grandchildren for Your Kingdom. Give me the strength to stand up for what's right and to speak out about injustices. Gift me with the courage to share the gospel of Jesus Christ, whether that's with my words specifically or by the way I live a life that's pleasing to You. Open my eyes to see what I can do or say that will point others to Jesus, most especially my own family. Let me be bold for You and help me to strengthen those in the trenches with me.

Amen.

Show your support of our country's military members. If you live near a base, find out how you can deliver homemade goodies to young sailors, soldiers, or Marines far from home with no family nearby. Look online to find different (reputable) sites that allow you to write military members overseas. And pray. Pray regularly for our military personnel and for their families.

CHAPTER TWENTY-EIGHT

A Chicken Sandwich for the Soul

"And whatever you do, do it heartily,
as to the Lord and not to men."
—Colossians 3:23 (NKJV)

It was so cold in Birmingham, Alabama, they had stuff shivering they didn't know could shake in the Deep South.

It was especially bitter on one January afternoon a few years back. And a good many folks had taken a respite from the cold by grabbing lunch at the Chick-fil-A on Highway 280 in Inverness.

One of the diners who came in that day was a bit unkempt. He was wearing jeans and a hoodie—hardly the kind of clothing for a day like that. Most folks just figured he was a homeless fellow.

The man first made eye contact with Mark Meadows, the owner of the Chick-fil-A. "I was about to leave when this gentleman walked in the door," Mark told me. "I could tell he needed some help. We have people come in from time to time—so you kind of know."

And sure enough, Mark's instinct was correct.

"He asked if there was some work he could do so that he could get something to eat," he said.

Now, it would not be unusual for a person like that be escorted out of a restaurant. But the Chick-fil-A on

Highway 280 is no ordinary restaurant. Last year, when a freak snowstorm hit the city, Meadows and his staff personally fed hundreds of motorists trapped in their cars—free of charge.

So instead of ordering the indigent man to leave, Mark invited him to have a meal. As the man waited for his chicken sandwich and waffle fries, Mark could not help but notice the man was rubbing his hands together.

"There's a look about somebody's hands that's been out in the cold," Mark said. "It's got that cold look about them." The man did not have a pair of gloves. So Mark gave him his.

"I went back and got his food and he put on the gloves and then he left," Mark said.

The entire encounter lasted just a few minutes—and that was that. But in this day and age of smart phones—that was not that.

Andrea Stoker happened to be eating lunch in the restaurant that day with her little boy. And she could not help but notice the interaction between the store owner and the disheveled man. She took a photograph and posted a message on her Facebook page—a message that has since gone viral.

Here's what she wrote:

"Bryson and I are sitting in Chick Fil A on 280. A man walked in to get warm with all of his earthly possessions on his back. The manager, who is on his break, got up and asked the man if he could get him anything. Before the man could even answer, the manager asked if the man had any gloves and handed him his, then got him the meal of his choice. There is still so much good in this world and I'm so grateful that Bryson saw it all unfold."

So why is Chick-fil-A so generous?

Well, Mark told me it's the same reason they gave away all those chicken sandwiches during last year's blizzard.

"It all comes from Truett Cathy and the Cathy family and the principles Chick-fil-A has been established on," he said.

And those principles are "to glorify God by being a faithful steward of all that is entrusted to us and to have a positive influence on all who come into contact with Chick-fil-A."

Folks, I've concluded that Chick-fil-A is a chicken sandwich for the soul.

No one quite knows for sure what happened to the young man who walked into the Chick-fil-A on that bitterly cold day. His whereabouts are something of a mystery.

"Do not forget to entertain strangers," Hebrews 13:2 (NKJV) reminds us. "For by doing so some have unwittingly entertained angels."

And some might have even served them a chicken sandwich and waffle fries.

1. The manager at that Chick-fil-A saw a need—and he did something about it. What can you learn from that?
2. A customer noticed his kindness to the indigent man. What would people see if they watched you?
3. How can showing kindness to someone lead people to Jesus?
4. How can you glorify God by being a faithful steward of the blessings He's given you?

Patriot Prayer

Father,

Give me eyes that will see the plight of others who are in need—and give me a heart that will always reply with kindness and compassion. Help me to remember that I might be the only one who speaks kindly to that person, supplies their need, and who cares about them as a human being. I imagine that they often feel invisible as people ignore them. Break my heart for that person. Help me to pray for them with tears on my cheeks, and help them to see the heart of Jesus in me. Let all that I do bring glory to You.

Amen.

It takes so little to show kindness to someone and, with a little planning, we can be ready when opportunities arrive. Sometimes just talking to that person and taking time to listen will touch them. Get some large zipper-style plastic bags and fill them with bottles of water, warm socks, a pair of gloves, lip balm for dry lips, and packs of peanut butter crackers and snack bars. Bibles and New Testaments are available at dollar stores. Buy some to include in the bags and keep some copies in your car so they're always available. And if the person is hungry, buy them something to eat. Do it as unto Jesus, and I promise you will always be the one who is most blessed.

Chicken Salad Ball

From the Kitchen of Michelle Cox

Ingredients:

8-ounce package cream cheese, softened
¼ cup Hellman's, Kraft, or other good-quality mayonnaise
2 tablespoons lemon juice
½ teaspoon salt
¼ teaspoon ground ginger
4 drops red pepper sauce
2 cups cooked chicken breast, finely chopped
1 ½ tablespoon onion, finely chopped (Vidalia or other sweet onion)
2 hard-boiled eggs, chopped
¾ cup finely-chopped pecans
Crackers

Directions:

Mix the cream cheese, mayonnaise, lemon juice, salt, ginger, and red pepper sauce until the mixture is smooth and blended. Gently add the chicken, chopped onion, and chopped hard-boiled eggs. Chill overnight and then shape into a ball or mold it into another specific shape if desired. Roll it in the chopped pecans. Serve with an assortment of crackers.

*I like to double the recipe and make three equally-sized balls. Then, I roll them in the chopped pecans. I line a long serving platter with green leaf lettuce and line up the three chicken salad balls in a row. Then, I surround them with strawberries and red and green grapes. It presents beautifully and people always come back for seconds.

Note: The first time I saw this recipe, I thought the ingredients were a little unusual. But thankfully, I'd already tasted it at an event, and it is so good!

CHAPTER TWENTY-NINE

On Wings Like Eagles

"But those who hope in the Lord will renew their strength. They will soar on wings like eagles; they will run and not grow weary, they will walk and not be faint."
—Isaiah 40:31 (NIV)

In the late 1700s, Benjamin Franklin, Thomas Jefferson, and John Adams worked to design an official seal for the newly formed nation of America. Though they struggled to come up with an idea that pleased Congress, parts of their design and those of two other committees were merged by Charles Thomson, the secretary of Congress, which resulted in an eagle as the focal point of the national seal.

With slight altering to replace a small white eagle with an American bald eagle, the seal was adopted to represent the United States of America, and the eagle became one of America's most iconic symbols. Committee members selected the eagle because it represented strength. The Founding Fathers and other committee members hoped to convey the strength of the new nation.

Isaiah 40:31 reminds us of our true hope, our only hope: the Lord. When we put our trust in God, when we hang onto Him and don't give up, when we stay strong because of His strength and not our own, then we will soar on the wings of eagles.

The eagle may be our nation's symbol—a representation of our country—but we can't put our hope in this great land of ours. We most certainly can and should love our country, but our hope doesn't lie in America. Our hope and faith must be rooted in the Lord for us to take wings and soar. Our loyalty and devotion must first be to Him. Then we can fight for our nation to return to God and fight for the next generation—our children and grandchildren—to turn their hearts back to the Lord.

Ephesians 6:10 (NIV) says, "Finally, be strong in the Lord and in his mighty power."

Friends, we need God's strength to turn our country around and to get back to the strong, mighty nation that we know we can be. We can't do this on our own. We need God. We can help those around us recognize God as our only hope for turning this nation around—to one that worships the Lord and chooses to put God first.

Reportedly, in a letter to his daughter, Benjamin Franklin complained about Congress's selection of the bald eagle as a national symbol. In his letter, Franklin referred to the bald eagle as "a Bird of bad moral Character."

Is that what's happened to our great nation? Have we become people of bad moral character? What can we do—what *must* we do—to get back to being a nation of strong moral values and principles? First, we should start with the person we see in the mirror each day. From there, changes need to spread to our family members, friends, and inner circle of companions. And after that, we hope for contagious changes to others around us.

Let's all soar with God's strength. It's our only hope.

Yankee Doodle

1. What do you think our country needs in order to soar again?
2. Why do you think the eagle symbolizes strength?
3. What do you see as the strengths of our country? The weaknesses?
4. When have you recently tapped into God's strength?

Patriot Prayer

Dear Father,

Our only hope is in You. When we put our hope and trust in You, rather than people or places, material wealth or things, when we truly admit and trust that You are all we need, then we can soar on the wings of eagles. Our strength lies in You alone. God, we are weak without You. And our country is weak without You. When we take You out of our country and deny Your Lordship, we falter. We were never meant to do this without You, dear Lord. Help us turn back to You and lean into Your strength. Guard us from arrogance, from thinking we can handle these trials our country is facing on our own. Let us be dependent on You, God, and Your strength.

Amen.

Our verse in Isaiah says we'll "walk and not grow faint" and we'll "run and not grow weary." With your family or an exercise buddy, plan to walk or run a different path several times a week. While walking or running, pray for the families who inhabit homes along the paths or businesses you encounter on the route. Pray for that community, and pray for the churches there. Choose an alternate path on another day and repeat.

CHAPTER THIRTY

A Firm Foundation

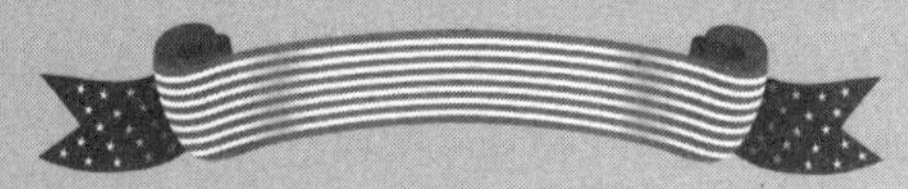

"He is like a man building a house, who dug deep and laid the foundation on the rock. And when the flood arose, the stream beat vehemently against that house, and could not shake it, for it was founded on the rock."
—Luke 6:48 (NKJV)

Just after my dishwasher turned my kitchen floor into a small stream, I noticed black spots edging the baseboards next to the faulty appliance. "I'd better call our insurance company," I told my husband. "We may need to replace the baseboards."

Well, I was right. The baseboards needed replacing. But so did my entire kitchen floor. The stream of water above was nothing compared to the river that flooded the foundation of our house, damaging the floor and destroying the crawl space insulation. Our house was compromised and needed much repair to restore its solid foundation.

Friends, the climate of our nation is compromised and has been for quite some time. We're on a shaky foundation, and we've caused the damage ourselves through the polarization of parties, the bitterness in our hearts for fellow brothers and sisters, the selfishness and greed lurking in our thoughts, and the negativity at every turn.

We've weakened the foundation with each ugly word, every mean thought, and all the hateful actions we've slung in the direction of others. And most significantly, with each step we take away from the Lord, we've chiseled and jack-hammered the foundation into fragile cracks and fractured crumbles.

Luke 6:46–49 (NIV) goes like this: "Why do you call me, 'Lord, Lord,' and do not do what I say? As for everyone who comes to me and hears my words and puts them into practice, I will show you what they are like. They are like a man building a house, who dug down deep and laid the foundation on rock. When a flood came, the torrent struck that house but could not shake it because it was well built. But the one who hears my words and does not put them into practice is like a man who built a house on the ground without a foundation. The moment the torrent struck that house, it collapsed and its destruction was complete."

It took months to repair my kitchen floor and baseboards, to shore up the foundation of our home, and replace the crawl space insulation. My family resides on a firm foundation again. In much the same manner, our nation needs to shore up our foundation by hearing God's Word and putting it into practice.

We can seal the cracks when we hide God's Word in our hearts. We need to dig deep and lay our foundation on the solid rock—on Jesus. Our hope truly is built on the blood of Jesus and His righteousness. We must turn back to God and lean into His firm foundation, or we'll never withstand the force of the storms.

Yankee Doodle

1. What makes you feel like our nation is on shaky ground? In what ways do you see evidence of America's firm foundation?
2. What practical steps can you take within your own family to "firm up" your foundation with God?
3. In Psalm 18:2, David calls the Lord his rock and fortress. How is God your fortress in troubling times?
4. Jesus said in Matthew 7 that the wise listen to and follow His teachings. Are you faithful to read God's Word regularly? Do you strive to follow Jesus's teachings?

Patriot Prayer

Dear Jesus,

Guide my family and help us strive to shore up and rebuild our foundation in You. Let us dig deep and secure ourselves in You, our solid rock, and cling to Your words and Your teachings. The only way my family and this nation can withstand the violent, vehement storms that are taking place every day before our very eyes is to hang onto You as our Savior, the light of the world, our hope for tomorrow, and our firm foundation. Seal the cracks and strengthen the broken parts of our nation, Jesus. Help me to do my part to teach the next generation about You, because You are our unshakable foundation.

Amen.

Sometimes illustrated messages make us see things in a fresh new way. Your assignment today is to get outside and play in the mud. Find a puddle, gather some sticks, rocks, and disposable cups, and teach a lesson from Luke 6 to your kids or grandkids. Build a stick house in the mud and pour a "torrent" of water from the cup. Watch the house crumble. Use large rocks to support the sticks (you may have to push them into the mud and squish the rocks tightly together to help them stand), pour water on top, and discuss the results.

CHAPTER THIRTY-ONE

From Sea to Shining Sea

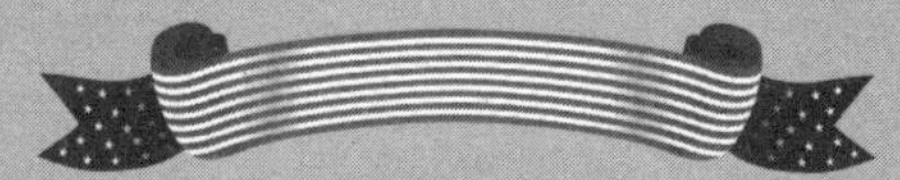

"Have we not all one father? Hath not one God created us? Why do we deal treacherously every man against his brother, by profaning the covenant of our fathers?"
—Malachi 2:10 (KJV)

The daughter of an economically-strapped truck driver and a stay-at-home mama, the young woman dreamed of seeing the world, from one coast to the other and beyond.

God heard the whispers of her "I want to see the world!" dream and turned them into reality when her husband joined the Navy after they both completed their Masters Degrees. But she was terrified to leave her place of birth—the only dot on the globe she'd ever known—and the comfort and security of her people.

Would she fit in? She'd always heard people were so different in other places.

Thankfully, they *were* different. In the most intelligent, warm, unique, fascinating ways. Ways in which she'd never dreamed from her tiny little dot on the globe. And they were the same. In the most loving, kind-hearted, interesting ways.

She found her people in Jacksonville, Florida with their first move. She found a brotherhood—sisterhood, rather—at Camp LeJeune, North Carolina. And more friends in Stafford, Virginia.

But that was the East Coast, the Atlantic Ocean. She'd most definitely heard folks were different on the West Coast. Fortunately, she found her different-yet-same sisterhood in Oceanside, California and her people in Poulsbo, Washington—on the Pacific Ocean.

From sea to shining sea, her sisterhood and brotherhood of peeps were unique and wonderful, challenging and rude, different and kind, the same and ornery, fascinating and beautiful. You know what remained consistent? From ocean to ocean and beyond, God created every single person. From coast to coast, we all have one Father—the Lord Almighty.

Why are we fighting brother against brother, sister against sister?

Yes, we're different in unique and wonderful ways, but the best similarity we share is our Heavenly Father. In 1 John 4:20 (ESV) it says, "If anyone says, 'I love God,' and hates his brother, he is a liar; for he who does not love his brother whom he has seen cannot love God whom he has not seen."

Hebrews 13:1 (ESV) tells us, "Let brotherly love continue."

Poet Katharine Lee Bates wrote the hymn "America the Beautiful" in 1893, asking God to shed His grace on

America and to reward this country with a true brotherhood that stretches from sea to shining sea.

God has answered the prayers of hymn singers from across our great land and given America more grace than we could ever deserve. God also rewarded us with brotherhood and yet, we seem to be trying every way possible to destroy that brotherhood.

Friends, let's show God how grateful we are for His grace by loving our brothers and sisters. From sea to shining sea—and beyond.

Yankee Doodle

1. How can knowing we all have the same Father help you treat others with kindness and love instead of animosity and bitterness?
2. The lyrics of "America the Beautiful" ask God to take our flaws and mend them. What are some of America's flaws that you can mend personally?
3. How have you felt God's grace and presence in the places you've lived?
4. What parts of America do you think are the most beautiful? Have you thanked God for that beauty?

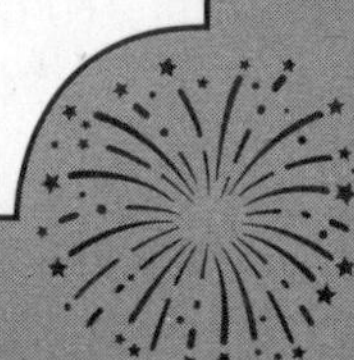

PATRIOT PRAYER

Dear Father,

Thank You for shedding Your amazing grace on our great country. We admit that we've turned a blind eye to Your goodness and blessings to our nation. Make us mindful of all that You've done for America. Help us restore the brotherhood—and sisterhood—of our blessed nation. Help us remember that You created us all, and we all have the same Father. Let us treat one another like brothers and sisters, despite our unique differences. We're all created in Your image, Lord God, no matter how different we look on the outside nor how we think and feel on the inside. Put us back together as a nation who welcomes the reward of brotherhood. We love You, Lord.

Amen.

Share the words of "America the Beautiful" with your kids and grandkids. Learn the lyrics of the song and sing it together or sing along with a recording of the song on your phone. Memorize the words of the song and ask each member of your family to commit to praying for God's continued grace on America.

CHAPTER THIRTY-TWO

A School That Teaches Kids Freedom Isn't Free

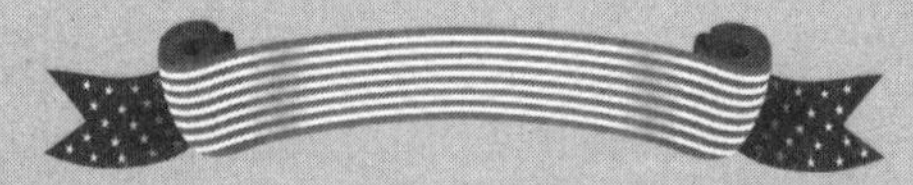

"Greater love hath no man than this, that a man lay down his life for his friends."
—John 15:13 (KJV)

Andrew Burns grew up in New Jersey. He worked in the World Trade Center. Some of his friends died in the terrorist attacks of September 11, 2001. Mr. Burns eventually moved to Greenwood Village, Colorado where he got a job teaching social studies to eighth graders. But the events of that day so many years ago made a profound impact on the school teacher.

"Some of my friends died on 9/11 and I want my kids to know that freedom isn't free," he told me. "I just love America. I love the freedom I have here and I know it wasn't free."

And that is the lesson he teaches eighth graders for an entire year—a simple phrase written on a chalkboard: freedom isn't free. The students spend the rest of the year proving the statement.

"I want the next generation of kids to learn that (freedom is not free)," he said. You see the World War II generation passing away and the sacrifices an entire generation made to preserve peace. Those who are serving today and have served continue to provide for us. The kids have got to know that."

Mr. Burns teaches his kids about the American Revolution and the Civil War. On Veteran's Day, a service member visits the classroom to talk about life in the military. They send care packages to our troops in Iraq and Afghanistan. And they even raised money to buy a puppy for a veteran suffering from PTSD.

"That's been our service project for the last few years," he said on my radio show. "We're up to about four puppies."

Now, many of you may be pleasantly dumbfounded right about now. A public school that actually teaches kids to love America and to respect our military? It's a beautiful thing.

But there's more to this classroom lesson about patriotism, and you might want to secure a handkerchief.

As part of their curriculum, school children would visit nearby Fort Logan National Cemetery—the final resting place for many of our fallen heroes. And Mr. Burns could not think of a more poignant place to conduct the last day of class on the last day of school: freedom isn't free.

Standing among the fallen soldiers, the students read the Gettysburg Address and Walt Whitman's "O Captain! My Captain!" They learn about the history of the cemetery and participate in a flag-folding ceremony.

"We talk about the solemnity of the place and have the kids look around and see the uniformity of the headstones and to see that this is the cost of freedom," Mr. Burns said.

This is the cost of freedom.

One by one, the eighth graders walk among the fallen, placing more than 4,000 American flags at the headstones of our heroes.

"It's the last lesson of the year," he explained. "We take the students to Fort Logan National Cemetery to put an exclamation point on that message."

A few days after I interviewed Mr. Burns, I received a message from one of my listeners. It turned out his father had been buried at Fort Logan and students at West Middle had placed a flag at his dad's headstone.

"I would like to thank you for such a wonderful thing to do for the students, community, and veterans at rest," the man wrote.

Longtime listeners of my radio show know there are a lot of things wrong in American public schools. But in Greenwood Village, Colorado, there is a public school that is doing something right.

The Bible emphasizes the importance of teaching our history to future generations. Our children and grandchildren need to know about their Christian heritage.

In Isaiah 46:9 (NIV), the prophet Isaiah admonished us, asking us to "remember the former things, those of long ago; I am God, and there is no other; I am God, and there is none like me."

We live in the greatest nation in the history of the world—an exceptional nation. We are that shining city on a hill, a beacon of hope for people seeking freedom.

And we have a responsibility to teach future generations that our freedom comes with a price—paid for by our fellow countrymen—who voluntarily put their lives on the line to defend the constitution.

President Reagan once said freedom is just one generation away from extinction. But I believe the republic is going to be just fine so long as we have teachers like Andrew Burns and academic institutions like West Middle School teaching future generations that freedom isn't free.

Yankee Doodle

1. The Bible tells us to "remember the former things." Why is it so important for us to remember the former things that have happened in our country?

2. Mr. Burns is teaching his students to become good citizens. How can that tie into our faith?

3. Why is it so important for us to teach future generations about the price of freedom?

4. Our brave men and women in the military have voluntarily—and sacrificially—given their lives for our freedom. And Jesus voluntarily—and sacrificially—gave His life so that we could have salvation and forgiveness for our sins. What do those sacrifices mean to you?

Patriot Prayer

Father,

Sometimes we forget what a great price has been paid for the things that we hold dear. Thank You for giving Your life for us. Such love is more than my mind can comprehend, but I'm grateful. Thank You for those who have fought for our country, who paid the ultimate sacrifice so that we could be free. May we never forget what they've done for our great nation. And, Lord, thank You for teachers who love this great land, who are teaching their students to love and cherish America, and to understand the great price that has been paid for the freedoms we enjoy each day. We are blessed beyond words.

Amen.

Make time to teach your children and grandchildren about what has led to our greatness as a country. Teach them the history of our country. Teach them to love America and to respect our flag. And make time to teach them about their spiritual heritage as well. Tell them about your salvation experience. Take them to the churches that have impacted your family. Share with them about the people who have inspired you to serve God. Tell your children and grandchildren the stories of faith from their ancestors who came before them, and how their faithfulness to God touched you. Then inspire the next generation to carry the torch of faith and freedom to another generation.

Sausage Balls

From the Kitchen of Michelle Cox

Ingredients:

2 packets (2 ¼ cups) Bisquick
2/3 cups milk
1 cup cheddar cheese, shredded
1 package Rudy's Farm, Swaggerty's, or other quality sausage

Stir together the Bisquick and the milk. Add the cheddar cheese and the sausage (which has been chopped into smaller pieces). Combine until well blended. (I usually do this by hand.) Make into balls a little bit larger than a melon ball. Bake on a greased cookie sheet at 400 degrees for 10–15 minutes or until browned. This will yield about 45 sausage balls.

*If you're in a hurry, make them into larger balls, flatten them a bit, and then bake a little longer until browned.

**The great news? They can be made ahead and frozen. Make as directed above, but don't bake them. Place the sausage balls on a cookie sheet and place it (covered) in the freezer until they are completely frozen. Store in a zipper-type freezer bag and use as needed. They don't have to be thawed. Just bake a bit longer until browned.

Note: These are awesome for a finger food, breakfast, snack, or whenever.

CHAPTER THIRTY-THREE

A Rose By Another Name

"But seek first the kingdom of God and His righteousness, and all these things shall be added to you."
—Matthew 6:33 (NKJV)

Do you have roses growing in your yard? I'm always fascinated by their beauty. Not just their spectacular colors, but the aroma is just divine. Don't you think? And those delicate petals. So pretty. Now, the thorns? That's a different story. I learned in my science classes as a kid that those prickles keep animals, like rabbits and deer, from decimating the plant of leaves and flowers. Later, I also learned the thorns help the plant cling to other vegetation so that it doesn't droop and break the stems.

Song of Solomon 2:1 mentions the "Rose of Sharon" and although that's the only place this phrase is mentioned in the Bible, the Rose of Sharon is often associated with Jesus. A region east of the Jordan River, the district of Sharon symbolizes beauty, purity, and love. Some believe the rose is the most perfect of all flowers.

The connection between the verse in Song of Solomon and Jesus embraces several layers, but one can certainly grasp the perfect Savior God sent to die for our sins and to purify us for a relationship with God. And what a beautiful relationship that is, right?

The national flower of the United States happens to be the rose. I doubt anyone made an association with the Rose of Sharon when making this choice, but I think it's quite fitting. Our country functions best when the Rose of Sharon—Jesus Christ—is Lord of our lives. When everything we do reflects a life focused on Him and how He would have us live.

The problem is, we've lost that focus in our country. Self-centeredness and entitlement run rampant instead. We don't seem to ponder what Jesus would do. Rather, we make choices and decisions out of selfishness and greed. We seek answers anywhere but the Bible. We turn to misplaced heroes and idols instead of the One who truly deserves our worship and adoration. Friends, I'm stepping on my own toes here, because I'm guilty of filtering my thoughts and decisions on what pleases me, what makes me happy, and what works best for me and my family.

Each day, I need the beauty and aroma of a life lived in Christ. The only way to get rid of my selfishness is to keep my focus on Jesus, the Rose of Sharon. I do love my country with passion and gusto, but the rose of America isn't my salvation. Only Jesus is.

Yes, our country has its share of thorns and prickles. Sometimes that prickle is the neighbor down the street and sometimes the thorn is the grouchy salesclerk. More often, though, I suspect that pokey person is me.

Let's clean up our own garden first, cling to the Rose of Sharon, and pray for the beautiful soul of our great country.

Yankee Doodle

1. What do you find the most beautiful about your relationship with Christ?
2. What does the aroma of Christ mean to you?
3. If you had to pick America's best quality, what would you choose? What do you see as the quality where America has the most need for improvement?
4. How can you celebrate America's best quality? How can you do your part to work on America's worst quality?

Patriot Prayer

Dear God,

America the beautiful is my country and I love her dearly. But we're not the country we used to be. We have turned away from You and put other people and things first in our lives. Help me change that in my own life first. Show me how to put Jesus first. Change my heart such that my thoughts and words and actions change, too. Help me to work sincerely on those changes and let them reflect You to everyone around me. Show me how to encourage others to turn back to Jesus, the Rose of Sharon. Prune our country, Lord. Pull up and destroy roots tethered to anything but You. May we once again be the beautiful nation that You desire.

Amen.

Think of someone you struggle to get along with because of their prickly nature. Perhaps you disagree politically. Maybe your religious beliefs conflict. Plan to purchase a potted plant with miniature roses or flowers to share with this person. Buy two, one for you to keep and one for that person. Use your plant as a visible reminder to pray for that person regularly—and to pray for our country. Let the beauty of the plant also remind you to keep your thorns—your own self-centeredness and entitlement in check.

CHAPTER THIRTY-FOUR

The United States of America

"Live in harmony with one another. Do not be proud, but be willing to associate with people of low position. Do not be conceited. Do not repay anyone evil for evil. Be careful to do what is right in the eyes of everyone. If it is possible, as far as it depends on you, live at peace with everyone."
—Romans 12:16–18 (NIV)

Two neighbors on our street in North Carolina were polar opposites. From hairstyles to church affiliations to political parties to parenting choices, Joe and Morgan couldn't agree on any subject. Both were very vocal about their beliefs and ideologies. They could rarely be in the same room without a heated argument. Thus, the entire neighborhood knew they couldn't be invited to the same block party.

That all changed during a wicked storm in the midst of hurricane season.

High-speed winds and torrential rain ripped off a corner of Joe's roof. When Morgan spotted Joe's frantic attempt to secure a tarp over the damaged section, Morgan donned a raincoat and hat, grabbed a ladder, and made his way into Joe's yard. With few words exchanged, the two men united to fight the vicious wind, instead of each other, to nail down the tarp. Soon, two other neighbors joined Joe and Morgan to complete the job.

With a handshake and a "thank you," the former enemies parted ways. Soon, Joe and Morgan began to nod to one another if they passed on opposite sidewalks. Eventually, one waved to the other. Before long, the two men spoke while collecting their mail, which hadn't happened in years because they made sure to avoid close contact.

It took months, but the two men figured out how to be cordial. Joe and Morgan would never boast BFF status, but under a category two hurricane, the two formed a unique friendship.

Do you know a Joe and Morgan kind of contentious relationship? Are *you* Joe or Morgan?

Friends, our country seems to delight in picking people apart these days because of subtle or huge differences. We tear each other down on social media for the smallest distinctions. We can't like someone if they don't look and act just like us or believe the same things we do. When did we get so self-centered that we can't seem to get along with anyone?

God certainly doesn't expect us to compromise our beliefs or go against His Word. But He does want us to live in harmony and peace with our brothers and sisters in this nation. He doesn't just want that, He demands that in today's verse. "If it is possible, as far as it depends on you, live at peace."

Live at peace. Live in harmony. Live united.

We will always have our differences in the United States of America. That's part of the beauty of our country.

But it doesn't mean we have to act ugly and mistreat our neighbors and friends. God doesn't want that. Our Founding Fathers didn't want that.

Let's unite for the common good of our country and love one another accordingly.

Yankee Doodle

1. Do you struggle to get along with people who seem different from you?
2. Think of that person with whom you have a contentious relationship. What can you do to live at peace with that person?
3. How can you live in harmony with others without compromising your beliefs?
4. What do you think it will take to unite our country?

Patriot Prayer

Dear God,

Sometimes it's hard for me to get along with those who think differently than me or those whose beliefs are the polar opposite of mine. Show me how to stay true to my beliefs and obey Your words in Scripture but to treat others with kindness and compassion simultaneously. Father, help us figure out how to unite our country for the good of our nation. We're always going to have differences, but can You please show us how to harness those qualities to make this an even better nation? Turn our hearts toward You. Give us the common bond of recognizing You as our Heavenly Father. Help us to see your unshakable love for us, and let us then share Your love with those around us.

Amen.

When you meet someone new who is quite different from you, make an effort to learn more about those differences before forming adverse feelings toward that person. Research (or even ask that person) about that issue seemingly dividing the two of you and see if you can find any commonalities. Educate yourself, pray over the differences, and find ways to live in harmony and peace—even if you still believe differently. You can love the person without loving how they believe.

CHAPTER THIRTY-FIVE

Proclaim Liberty

"For you were called to freedom, brothers and sisters; only do not turn your freedom into an opportunity for the flesh, but serve one another through love. For the whole Law is fulfilled in one word, in the statement, 'YOU SHALL LOVE YOUR NEIGHBOR AS YOURSELF.'"

—Galatians 5:13–14 (NASB)

Have you ever seen the Liberty Bell in Philadelphia, Pennsylvania? What do you remember from history classes about the bell? If you're like me, you're probably cringing just a bit because you're trying to remember those dates we had to select from a multiple-choice list and the creators' names we had to scribble in the blanks.

But are you also like me in that you don't remember being taught the significance of the inscription on the bell?

The gist of the history of the Liberty Bell goes like this. The State House bell, as it was originally called, was commissioned for the tower of the Pennsylvania State House to call in lawmakers for meetings back in the mid-1700s. The Speaker of the Pennsylvania Assembly, Isaac Norris, commissioned these words as an inscription for the bell: "Proclaim Liberty Throughout All the Land Unto All the Inhabitants Thereof."

Do you know where those words come from? Leviticus 25:10 (KJV), that's where.

At its inception, an iconic American symbol—often used politically to extol the virtues of liberty as it relates to opposing parties and oppressed people groups—was meant to uphold God's Word and celebrate religious freedoms.

Why are we guilty in our nation of taking the glory away from God? Why do we continuously take God out of the equation and elevate man instead?

Friends, there's only one way to be truly free, and that's by accepting Jesus as our Lord and Savior. The Bible says in John 8:36 (ESV), "So if the Son sets you free, you will be free indeed." Before that, John reminded us in chapter eight, verse thirty-two, "And you will know the truth, and the truth will set you free."

Sadly in our nation right now, falsehoods and untruths run rampant. There's fake news and slanted news and blatant lies. Most of those deceits fall in direct opposition of God, the Father of truth. We have to stop the lies and stand for truth.

We as a nation should expect truthfulness, starting with friends and neighbors, and rallying to community, state, and national leaders, and then blasting onto the pages or pictures of every form of media outlets.

Knowing Jesus as our personal Savior and hanging onto God's truths from His Word is the only way we'll ever be truly free, my friends. Sharing Jesus with others who don't know Him and serving those who adamantly oppose us (by showing them the love of Jesus) can pull our nation back together so we can truly ring the bell of freedom again.

Yankee Doodle

1. What does it mean to you to be free in Christ?
2. How does freedom in Christ spill over into the political arena?
3. How do you discern truthful media reporting? Are you willing to do your research before sharing something you heard that might not be accurate?
4. If you could inscribe a Bible verse onto an iconic American symbol to tell others about true freedom and liberty, which verse would you choose?

Patriot Prayer

Dear God,

You are the Father of truth. You are perfect and holy and good. There is no other God but You. Thank you, Father, for the truth of Your Word. Every verse and passage speaks of Your goodness and truth. Lord, I am so grateful for the freedom You have given me through Your Son, Jesus Christ. I thank You for the freedoms You've mercifully given our great nation and plead with You to help us turn back to You so that we can be worthy of those liberties again. Please thwart the instigator of lies and help our nation be mindful of deceit and inaccuracies from the enemy. Help us to look to You alone for truth and true freedom.

Amen.

Do your homework and research the media outlets you trust for news and information. Can you vet each one as an accurate disseminator of facts and not lies or simply opinions? Plan to challenge information given to you by others that you believe could be inaccurate. Be willing to find answers with and for that person to stop the falsehoods and perpetuate truth instead.

CHAPTER THIRTY-SIX

"PUFF GRAHAM"

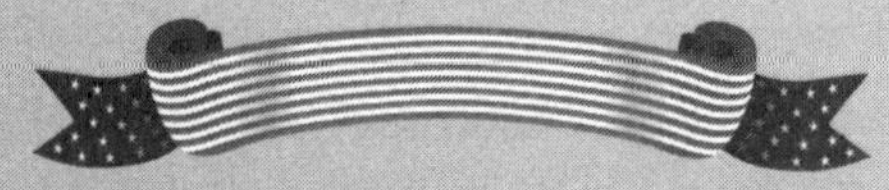

"And we know that all things work together for good to them that love God, to them who are the called according to his purpose."
—Romans 8:28 (KJV)

Throughout time, God has used the most unusual people to accomplish his mission. The same is true for America's pastor, Billy Graham.

The lanky young man from North Carolina with the blond hair and booming voice was not always a household name. But that all changed in the Spring of 1949.

Graham and his evangelistic team launched a series of revival meetings in Los Angeles. They erected a massive tent that would eventually seat up to 7,000 people. It was called the "Canvas Cathedral."

William Randolph Hearst, the great media tycoon, got wind of Graham's crusade and dispatched reporters and photographers to cover the proceedings.

Hearst directed his staff to send a message to every news outlet he owned across the country: "Puff Graham." And within a matter of days, Hearst-owned newspapers across the nation had front-page headlines promoting or "puffing" the news about the Canvas Cathedral.

Randall King, writing in the *Journal of Church and State*, recounted the aftermath of those stories: "In a Los

Angeles revival that included the conversion of Hollywood stars, Graham was surprised by a crowd of reporters and photographers one night shortly before the service. When Graham asked what caused the fuss, a reporter said, 'You have just been kissed by William Randolph Hearst.'"

It was supposed to be a three-week crusade, but the response to the gospel message was so great that it was extended by five weeks. Among those who came to know Christ were many well-known sports figures and Hollywood stars.

And that's how Billy Graham's journey to becoming America's pastor began—thanks to the generosity of a man who bought printer's ink by the barrel.

Hearst was not known to be a religious man, so it's unclear why he was so attracted to the young evangelist. Some speculated it could have been Graham's vehement opposition to Communism and his outright red-white-and-blue patriotism. Such ideals were shared by the newspaper publisher.

"Hearst and I did not meet, talk by phone, or correspond as long as he lived," Graham wrote in his memoir, *Just as I Am*.

Billy Graham would go on to preach the gospel to hundreds of millions of people around the globe. He became a respected counselor to many American presidents and, in times of great crisis, he brought comfort to the nation.

God could have used any sort of vessel to magnify the ministry of Billy Graham. But He chose to use a newspaperman.

It seems an unlikely choice, especially in modern America when many newsrooms are not so friendly to people of faith. But it's a beautiful illustration of a moment in time when God used a newspaper tycoon to broadcast the Good News across the globe.

Yankee Doodle

1. Dr. Billy Graham had a heart to serve God and to impact his country for Him. God honored that and sent an unlikely source to expand Billy Graham's ministry. How does that inspire you for something you want to do for God?
2. A young boy who grew up on a dairy farm became a man who reached the world for God and also became a counselor to presidents. God used someone ordinary and made him extraordinary. What could God do with your life if you'd let Him?
3. Billy Graham has gone to be with Jesus now. He left some huge footsteps to fill. What could you do to help spread the gospel and to impact our country?
4. God sometimes uses unlikely people for His purposes. Are you willing to let God use you?

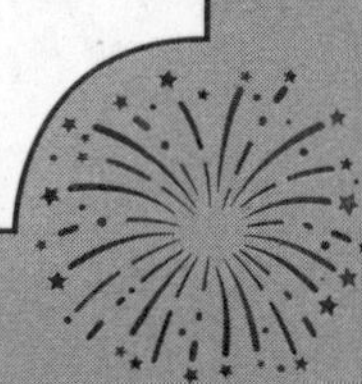

Patriot Prayer

Father,

You've specialized in using ordinary people for Your purposes. I sometimes feel as if I don't have much to offer to You or my country—but if You can use me, I'm Yours. Thank You for Billy Graham and his heart for You and for America. Thank You for his faithfulness—a faithfulness that literally touched the world—and my life. Help me to trust You as that lad with five smooth stones did. Help me to give You whatever I have that You can use—just as that little boy with five loaves and two fishes did. Help me to weep for my country until it turns back to You. Help me to make a difference.

Amen.

Take some time to reflect on what you have to offer to God and our country. Make a list. It might not seem like much to you, but God can do a lot with a willing heart. If all of us in our country did even a little to make America better and to reach our world for God, it would have a huge collective impact. I mean, think about what God did with a little boy's lunch—the one that fed 5,000 men, women, and children—and there were leftovers to spare.

Banana Bread

From the Kitchen of Mrs. Winn

Ingredients:

4 tablespoons buttermilk*
3 medium-sized ripe bananas, mashed well
½ cup canola or vegetable oil
1 teaspoon baking soda
1 ½ cups all-purpose flour
1 cup sugar
Pinch of salt
1 egg
½ cup pecans, chopped

Directions:

Preheat the oven to 350 degrees. Mix all the ingredients, blending well. Bake in a greased and floured loaf pan for 50 minutes or until golden brown.

*If you don't have buttermilk, you can add one tablespoon of lemon juice to a cup of milk, let it sit for five minutes, and then use four tablespoons.

CHAPTER THIRTY-SEVEN

It Was Almighty God

"'I am the Alpha and the Omega, the Beginning and the End,' says the Lord, 'who is and who was and who is to come, the Almighty.'"
—Revelation 1:8 (NKJV)

Picture this. Ninety-nine-year-old Abram is just minding his business in Canaan, and the Lord appears to chat with him. Can you even imagine how you might react to the Lord showing up while you're out wandering around, doing whatever ninety-nine-year-olds did back in biblical days?

And the first words the Lord spoke to Abram in Genesis 17:1 (NIV) must have reverberated for miles. "I am God Almighty; walk before me faithfully and be blameless."

God Almighty. Translated from the Hebrew words, *El Shaddai*. The God of Heaven as the God who is enough, sufficient to meet every need, the God of power and might.

The all-sufficient, powerful, mighty God tells Abram to walk before him faithfully. In other words, he needs to be in His presence at all times. And God tells him to be blameless. Does that mean Abram will sin no more? Obviously not, because that would be impossible, but our loving Father had a plan for our sinful human nature.

How have we come so far from God's desires for us as His created children and for us as a nation? What if

God appeared to each one of us and said, "Walk before me faithfully and be blameless?" Well, technically, He did. Through those words to Abram in Genesis 17, before discussing the new covenant with him, we as believers can recognize that God requires the same of us. To walk in His presence. To be faithful to Him and Him alone. To strive with every fiber of our being to live a blameless life, one of such admirable character as to be pleasing to the Lord.

In a verse in the last book of the Bible, God reminds us that He is the beginning and the end—the Almighty. From the first pages of Scripture, when God created the universe with His magnificent power to the covenant with Abram when God reveals his name, Almighty God, to the last pages of Scripture in Revelation, and every book in between, God reveals His might.

God Almighty can fix our nation, but we must—we absolutely *must*—walk in His presence and turn from our sin. We as a nation must stop denying that it was *God Almighty*. It was, and is, and will be to come. We can turn our hearts and minds back to Him. We can put Him first in our lives. We can recognize Him as the Almighty God that He is.

Friends, let's live in His presence and be blameless. It's our only hope to fix our nation.

Yankee Doodle

1. What does it mean to you to live blamelessly?
2. Do you have a tendency to blame *others* for the mess our nation is in?
3. Think about a time when God made His presence known to you. How did you feel about our Almighty God in that moment?
4. How does it comfort you that God is the beginning and the end?

Patriot Prayer

Father,

Guide me each day, from the moment my eyes open to the moment I shut them, to walk in Your presence. Counsel me to filter every thought, every word, and every action through Scripture so that I might live blamelessly before You. Help me to keep You at the forefront of my mind so that every decision I make reflects my love for You and my trust in You. Remind me daily that You are the beginning and end, the Alpha and Omega, so that I can know with certainty that You are always in control. You were, You are, and You will be. Allow me to focus on my own blame and sin so that I might repent and turn back to You.

Amen.

Look online to find the names of God as written in the Bible. Make a list of the names of God that resonate most with you and record the meaning of each name. You might even consider putting each name and meaning on separate index cards—somewhat like flash cards—and review them often. Use the list to help you pray in the morning when you wake up and glance back through the list at night to see how God showed up for you that day. And when you pray, don't forget to ask Almighty God to bring our country back to Him.

CHAPTER THIRTY-EIGHT

And That's the Truth

"Jesus said to him, 'I am the way, the truth, and the life. No one comes to the Father except through Me.'"
—John 14:6 (NKJV)

I've always been fascinated by holidays, particularly the odd and obscure ones. International Moment of Frustration Scream Day. Yeah, that's an odd one for sure. Ice Cream for Breakfast Day—now there's one I can get behind.

I found out something interesting about Independence Day. Did you know the Declaration of Independence wasn't actually signed on July 4th? The Continental Congress declared its freedom from Britain on July 2, 1776, but by the time the now-famous men signed the Declaration, the calendar had moved to August 2, 1776.

I bet you're thinking you'd like to go back and dispute the validity of a history test question or two, right? That got me thinking. Lately, it seems like we can get hung up on something we think is a fact, and we're willing to die on a hill for that belief.

Remember the old joke about the young homemaker cutting both ends off the ham before baking it, and when her new husband asked why she did it, she replied, "That's just how you bake a ham. My mama always did it that way."

So, she asked her mom the same question. Her mom said, "That's just how you bake a ham. My mama always did it that way."

So, she asked her grandma. And you know what she said? "I don't have a pan big enough for the ham to fit, so I cut off both ends first."

We get hung up on something we think is a fact, a truth, and we're willing to fight tooth and nail about that *truth*. The only truths we need to be willing to die on a hill for are the truths of the Bible. Jesus Christ is the way, the truth, and the life.

We can never forget that Jesus is our truth. He's worthy of our devotion and honor. He is worthy of our worship and praise. We owe our salvation to Jesus. That's the truth we need to fight for.

Before we dig our heels in and battle with someone on hearsay that we declare is absolute truth, we should dig deeper with due diligence, and find out just how accurate those things are. Maybe we should take it slow and hear someone out before we pass judgment.

Let's not budge on truth—on *the* Truth—but let's cool off before we get so hot under the collar that we're spewing bitterness and unkindness toward others. Let's save the fireworks for July Fourth, the actual-but-not-actual Independence Day, and stop using them on our brothers and sisters. We can do better, friends.

Yankee Doodle

1. How will sharing the truth of Jesus Christ turn our country around?
2. Who do you know that needs to know about Jesus? Have you invited that person to church or your home to talk about Him?
3. What truths of the Bible are most important to you?
4. How can you find ways to accept those who are not kind to you without compromising the truth of the Bible?

Patriot Prayer

Dear God,

Thank you for Jesus—the Way, the Truth, and the Life. Give me courage to be bold for Him. Help me to make His name known to others through my words and actions. Help me stand on truth, Lord, so I won't fall for inaccuracies and falsehoods. Help me to test the things I read and hear so that I might filter those things through Your truths. Keep me from digging my heels in about an unimportant issue that causes strife between me and another one of Your children. Keep my heart pure, God, and keep it focused on You. Turn my heart back to You. Turn this nation back to You. Forgive us, Lord, for how we have hurt You. Have mercy on us, God—even though we don't deserve it.

Amen.

Have you shared the fundamental truths of the Bible with your kids and grandkids? Fellow patriots, do your part to pass on the truths of God's Word to the next generation. Look online for "fundamental truths of the Bible" and make a list to share with family. List the biblical reference to go along with each truth and read the verses together as you discuss what God tells us in His Word.

CHAPTER THIRTY-NINE

Mansions and Palaces

"In my Father's house are many mansions: if it were not so, I would have told you. I go to prepare a place for you."
—John 14:2 (KJV)

Even though ours were the only two houses for miles on that country road, our families didn't mingle socially. I mean, after all, we lived in an old house with very meager means, and she lived in the mansion across the street, first with her husband and then as a widow. It certainly seemed like a mansion to me—a large, spacious two-story home with decorative columns, set away from the road down a long driveway lined with azaleas on either side.

Dr. Simmons, born in 1916, held the prestigious honor of being in the first class to which women were admitted to her university's school of medicine.

Across the street from her mansion sat my childhood home: a wood-framed farmhouse without central heat or air that the bank owned more than my father did.

I dreamed of a mansion like hers.

Did you know the White House originally went by the name "Presidential Palace" or "Executive Mansion?"

Every four years, two candidates vie for a position that will land them residential status in the Executive

Mansion. Lately, more so than ever before, that competition often results in name-calling, mud-slinging, false accusations, true but embarrassing accusations, bitterness, and a host of unkind words hurled randomly at fellow brothers and sisters.

In contrast, the only requirement for residential status in one of God's mansions is a willingness to welcome Jesus as Lord and Savior of our life. A *yes* to Jesus means an eternal life in Heaven with God. No more pain. An absence of tears and suffering. No name-calling, falsehoods, bitterness, or unkind words. Instead, an eternity of worshipping the God who loved us first. The One who loved us with such intensity and passion that He sent his only Son to die a miserable death on the cross for the forgiveness of sin—so that we could have life everlasting.

I don't know about you, but that's the mansion I want to call home. I want others to have the opportunity to call Heaven their home, too. Won't you join me in telling others about Jesus? Let's turn this nation back to God, with each person we meet, one person at a time.

I once saw this on someone's social media post: Let's make Heaven crowded. I know that's not really a thing—God has all that figured out. But isn't that a nice visual image?

Let's look forward to our heavenly mansion, and while we wait, let's work to make Heaven crowded.

Yankee Doodle

1. When you think about your mansion in Heaven, what does it look like to you?
2. Who in your circle of friends or acquaintances needs to hear about Jesus for the first time? Or maybe even the second or third time?
3. Think about someone you know personally with a very different lifestyle or opposing viewpoints. How would you feel if your heavenly mansion was right next to that person?
4. Have you made sure all of your extended family members know about the mansions in Heaven?

Patriot Prayer

Father,

Thank you for the promise of a mansion in Heaven. I'm so glad I know where my permanent home is, Lord. Thank you for sending Your Son to die on the cross for my sins. That sacrificial act opened the door for my mansion in eternity. Forgive me, Lord, for those times I selfishly keep Jesus to myself, for not being willing to tell others about their opportunity for a mansion by opening the door to Jesus as their Savior. And God, especially forgive me for those I meet whom I'm not sure I want sharing the neighborhood in Heaven with me. Show me how to boast about Jesus so much that I help others dream about their own mansion one day.

Amen.

Become informed about the current residents of the White House. Find out the names of those living in the residential area, but also research specific names of those who have offices in the West Wing or the East Wing. Make a list of as many names and titles as you can find. Take that list and pray often for those folks. Pray for their hearts to be aligned with God's truths.

CHAPTER FORTY

Ronald Reagan—Soul Winner

"For God so loved the world, that he gave his only begotten Son, that whosoever believeth in him should not perish, but have everlasting life."
—John 3:16 (KJV)

Karen Tumulty, a *Washington Post* journalist, had been researching a biography she was writing about the late First Lady Nancy Reagan when she came across a letter.

Tumulty had discovered the letter—dated August 2, 1982—tucked away at the Reagan Library in a cardboard box.

"I came across this truly extraordinary letter that President Reagan himself had written," she recalled.

Dr. Loyal Davis, his father-in-law, was in failing health. The renowned neurosurgeon was days away from death, and Reagan knew that he was not a follower of Christ.

So, on a Saturday afternoon at the White House, the president wrote a lengthy letter to Dr. Davis—pleading with him to consider surrendering his life to Jesus Christ.

Here's a portion of what Reagan wrote:

The apostle John said, "For God so loved the world that he gave his only begotten son that who so ever believed in him would not perish but have everlasting life."

We have been promised that all we have to do is ask God in Jesus name to help when we have done all we can — when we've come to the end of our strength and abilities and we'll have that help. We only have to trust and have faith in his infinite goodness and mercy.

Loyal, you and Edith have known a great love — more than many have been permitted to know. That love will not end with the end of this life. We've been promised this is only a part of life and that a greater life, a greater glory awaits us. It awaits you together one day and all that is required is that you believe and tell God you put yourself in his hands.

It's impossible for us to understand the high-pressure situations our presidents face every day in the Oval Office. Encountering the magnitude of being the leader of the free world and making life-and-death decisions every day. It's no wonder our leaders leave office with gray hair.

But the circumstances President Reagan faced as he penned the letter to his father-in-law were quite unique. Just seventeen months before, he had survived a would-be assassin's bullet. And on the world stage, Reagan was waging a fierce fight against the Soviet Union—a Cold War.

In spite of the global calamities, Reagan remained steadfast. He understood that the most pressing matter of the day was the state of his father-in-law's soul.

I thought it quite remarkable that President Reagan, writing on White House stationery, did not close his letter with a formal phrase. Instead, he simply signed it, "Love, Ronnie."

How many times have we found ourselves in the throes of adversity, when our circumstances seem hopeless? I wonder if we would have the same state of mind as Ronald Reagan? Even though he struggled through valleys, the Gipper always remembered that the main thing was the main thing.

Eleven days after Reagan wrote that letter, his father-in-law breathed his last breath. In later years, Nancy would say that her father did indeed turn to God. And for that we say, blessed assurance.

But the most poignant part of Ms. Tumulty's tender telling is that the most powerful man in the world set aside all of his troubles, "took pen in hand and set out on an urgent mission—to rescue one soul."

Yankee Doodle

1. Ronald Reagan greatly impacted our country. What part do you think his faith played in that?
2. The president of the United States took time to share the gospel with his father-in-law. Why do we so often neglect to do the same with others?
3. How do you think facing the assassin's bullet impacted Ronald Reagan's spiritual journey?
4. Sharing the gospel with others will impact their lives and the state of our nation. What can you do to become bolder about sharing your faith?

Patriot Prayer

Father,

I'm so grateful that it doesn't matter if we're the president of the United States or just an ordinary person—we can still impact lives for eternity. Give us boldness to share our faith. Give us hearts that are concerned for the state of someone else's soul. Help us not to wait until it's too late. Help us to equip ourselves to share about You. Give us hearts that will see others who need You. And if we will share the greatest message ever told, our country and our world will never be the same again.

Amen.

There is nothing that will impact our nation more than becoming a country that honors God. We have the best news in the world. It's time to quit treating it like a well-kept secret. The gospel changes people—and if we'll return to God, it will change our country. Friends, I want to see you in Heaven someday. I'll be there, not because of anything I've done, but because of what Jesus did on the cross. He wants you to come to Him. He loves you so much that He gave His life for you. Salvation is a free gift. You just need to accept it. All of us have sinned and done wrong—but Jesus paid the price for this with His life. If you don't know Him, pray today. Confess that you've sinned. Give your heart to Him and ask Him to be your Savior. You'll never make a better decision. May God bless you, dear ones, and may God bless America.

Bean's Peach Freezer Jam

From the Kitchen of Billie "Bean" Fulton

Ingredients:

2 cups of crushed fresh peaches
4 cups of sugar
1 drop of red food coloring (optional)
¾ cup cold water
1 box Sure-Jell
Pint jars, lids, and rings

Directions:

Peel the peaches, slice them, and then use a potato masher to crush them. Strain the juice off if needed. Add the four cups of sugar to the crushed peaches and mix well several times. Let rest for ten minutes while the sugar dissolves with the peaches. At the end of the time if the sugar is still gritty, mix again and let sit for five more minutes. If it's not a pretty peach color (and nobody is allergic to red food dye), you can add one drop of red food coloring to deepen the color.

In a saucepan, mix together ¾ cup of cold water and one box of Sure-Jell. Bring the mixture to a rolling boil, stirring constantly. Boil for one full minute.

Pour the hot mixture over the peaches and mix well. Ladle into pint jars, filling to ½ inch from the top. Put the lids and rings on the jars. The mixture should already be starting to jell. Label the jars and store in the freezer.

Bibliography

Abraham Lincoln Online. "Abraham Lincoln's House Divided Speech." *Abraham Lincoln Online*, n.d. https://www.abrahamlincolnonline.org/lincoln/speeches/house.htm.

Avalon Project. "First Inaugural Address of Dwight D. Eisenhower." *Yale Law School*, n.d. https://avalon.law.yale.edu/20th_century/eisen1.asp.

Chabad. "The Jewish Story of the UNC Frat Boys Who Held Up the American Flag." *Chabad.org*, n.d. https://www.chabad.org/news/article_cdo/aid/6428905/jewish/The-Jewish-Story-of-the-UNC-Frat-Boys-Who-Held-Up-the-American-Flag.htm.

Christian Citizen. "Our Country, May She Always Be in the Right." *Christian Citizen*, n.d. https://christiancitizen.us/our-country-may-she-always-be-in-the-right/.

Daily Tar Heel. "Vigil for Palestine." *The Daily Tar Heel*, May 2024. https://www.dailytarheel.com/article/2024/05/university-0430-vigil-for-palestine.

Facebook. "Chick-fil-A Manager Helps a Man in Need, and It Goes Viral." *Facebook*, n.d. https://www.facebook.com/IntelignMergedMedia/posts/chick-fil-a-manager-helps-a-man-in-need-and-it-goes-viral-lookingoutforoneanothe/1531623770451183/.

Focus on the Family. "When the President of the United States Was Baptized—Could It Happen Again?" *Daily Citizen*, n.d. https://dailycitizen.focusonthefamily.com/when-the-president-of-the-united-states-was-baptized-could-it-happen-again/.

Fox News. "Chick-fil-A Gives Free Food to Motorists Stranded in Southern Snowstorm." *Fox News*, n.d. https://www.foxnews.com/opinion/chick-fil-a-gives-free-food-to-motorists-stranded-in-southern-snowstorm.

———. "Trump Says Life Spared to Restore America's Greatness during Victory Speech." *Fox News*, n.d. https://www.foxnews.com/politics/trump-says-life-spared-restore-america-greatness-during-victory-speech.

———. "Todd Starnes: West Middle School in Greenwood Village, Colorado, at Fort Logan National Cemetery." *Fox News*, n.d. https://www.foxnews.com/opinion/todd-starnes-west-middle-school-greenwood-village-colorado-fort-logan-national-cemetary.

Founders Online. "From James Madison to William Bradford, 9 November 1772." *National Archives*, n.d. https://founders.archives.gov/documents/Madison/01-01-02-0015.

———. "To Abigail Adams from John Adams, 3 July 1776." *National Archives*, n.d. https://founders.archives.gov/documents/Adams/04-02-02-0016.

GodVine. "Chick-fil-A Manager's Touching Act of Kindness for a Homeless Man." *GodVine*, n.d. https://www.godvine.com/read/chick-fil-a-managers-touching-act-of-kindness-for-a-homeless-man-802.html.

Hillsdale Free Methodist Church. "Reagan's Letter." *Hillsdale FMC*, n.d. https://hillsdalefmc.net/reagans-letter/.

Lincoln Online. "Abraham Lincoln's House Divided Speech." *Abraham Lincoln Online*, n.d. https://www.abrahamlincolnonline.org/lincoln/speeches/house.htm.

Los Angeles Times. "William Randolph Hearst's Influence on Evangelism." *Los Angeles Times*, June 7, 1997. https://www.latimes.com/archives/la-xpm-1997-06-07-me-1034-story.html.

Matthew Fox. "Bonhoeffer & Aquinas on How Silence Feeds Evil & Becomes Evil." *Daily Meditations with Matthew Fox*, November 19, 2021. https://dailymeditationswithmatthewfox.org/2021/11/19/bonhoeffer-aquinas-on-how-silence-feeds-evil-becomes-evil/.

National Archives. "Declaration of Independence: Full Transcript." *National Archives*, n.d. https://www.archives.gov/founding-docs/declaration-transcript.

New Jersey Government. "Ben Franklin and the Delaware River." *New Jersey Government*, n.d. https://www.nj.gov/drbc/basin/living/benfranklin.html.

Pondering Principles. "Quotes by John Jay." *Pondering Principles*, n.d. https://ponderingprinciples.com/quotes/jay/.

Premier Christian News. "'Make America Pray Again': Donald Trump Becomes a Bible Seller." *Premier Christian News*, n.d. https://premierchristian.news/en/news/article/make-america-pray-again-donald-trump-becomes-a-bible-seller.

Reading Religion. "The Religious Journey of Dwight D. Eisenhower." *Reading Religion*, n.d. https://readingreligion.org/9780802878731/the-religious-journey-of-dwight-d-eisenhower/.

Reagan Library. "Remarks at the Annual National Prayer Breakfast." *Reagan Library Archives*, n.d. https://www.reaganlibrary.gov/archives/speech/remarks-annual-national-prayer-breakfast-1.

Sun Herald. "Military Honors in Mississippi." *Sun Herald*, n.d. https://www.sunherald.com/news/local/military/article123524654.html.

Todd Starnes. "Brave Young Men: UNC Chancellor Saves Old Glory from Violent Mob." *Todd Starnes*, n.d. https://www.toddstarnes.com/campus/brave-young-men-unc-chancellor-save-old-glory-from-violent-mob/.

UNC Alumni. "Fraternity Members Speak at Republican Convention." *UNC Alumni*, n.d. https://alumni.unc.edu/news/fraternity-members-speak-at-republican-convention/.

Washington Post. "A Lost Letter from Ronald Reagan to His Dying Father-in-Law Shows the President's Faith." *Washington Post*, September 14, 2018. https://www.washingtonpost.com/opinions/a-lost-letter-from-ronald-reagan-to-his-dying-father-in-law-shows-the-presidents-faith/2018/09/14/5aaab8c0-b140-11e8-9a6a-565d92a3585d_story.html.

WYFF 4. "William Randolph Hearst Gives Billy Graham's Ministry a Boost." *WYFF 4*, n.d. https://www.wyff4.com/article/william-randolph-hearst-gives-graham-s-ministry-boost/6997059.

X (formerly Twitter). Elon Musk. "Tweet." May 2024. https://x.com/elonmusk/status/1792759443593351262?mx=2.

Acknowledgments

I want to thank my wonderful team at Starnes Media Group—some of the most dedicated broadcasters and journalists in the country. Dalton, thank you for always having my back. Grace, Ben, Dylan, Gene, Kristin, Sheryl, and Caleb—you guys are the best! I also want to thank the great team at Post Hill Press and the crew at Newsmax television. I could not write a single word without the prayer support from my church family. And my sweet family—patriots all!

—Todd

I want to thank my husband, Paul, for his encouragement, prayers, and help around the house as I work to meet deadlines. Thank you to our agents, Tamela Hancock Murray and Dalton Glasscock for all your help with contracts. You are both dear friends. Sylvia Schroeder, we're grateful for your assistance with this book and for your friendship. Thank you to Anthony Ziccardi and the staff at Post Hill Press. You are amazing and it's always a joy to work with you. And I'm so grateful for the wonderful friends who pray so faithfully for me and my work. I couldn't do what I do without you. You are such an encouragement and I love you. Finally, thank You, Lord, for allowing me to write for You.

—Michelle

About the Authors

Todd Starnes is a Newsmax host and national radio show host. He's an award-winning journalist and the owner of KWAM, a news radio station in Memphis, Tennessee. Todd serves on the board of directors of the Tennessee Association of Broadcasters.

Michelle Cox is an award-winning and bestselling author of thirty-eight books, including the *When God Calls the Heart* series of devotional books, based on the *When Calls the Heart* television series, Hallmark's #1 show. She's been a guest on numerous radio and television shows, is a popular speaker and conference instructor, and has also written for Focus on the Family, Guideposts, FoxNews.com, Christian Cinema, and many other publications and sites.